Heartfelt Endorsements

On the outside, most people's lives look normal and good, if not enviable, compared to ours. What is true, however, is the outside often hides heartache and, on some occasions, brutality, abuse, and loneliness. David Zailer invites us inside his family story and brilliantly describes what it is like to live under the withering presence of a gifted and cruel narcissist who is beloved and respected in the church. How does one live with the ugly contradiction when faith is highjacked by religiosity to cover abuse? How does one grow to love the truth when truths are used to camouflage lies? His heroic tale of coming back to himself and greater truths is a wild, compelling, and hope-filled ride. The vistas you will see while you ride with David on his motorcycle are a vision of what redemption can look like if you can tell the truth and keep pursuing goodness despite the cost.

DAN AND BECKY ALLENDER | Professor of Counseling Psychology and Co-founders of The Allender Center for Trauma and Abuse at The Seattle School of Theology and Psychology

So many of us will, at one time or another, have blithely sung along to the Sunday school song "hide it under a bushel, no! I'm gonna let it shine" in blissful ignorance of the strength it takes to be vulnerable and let your light shine. In beautiful prose, with searing honesty, David lets his light shine in the pages of this book. In doing so, he also invites the reader to face their triumphs, tragedies, and heartfelt truths. Describing his own spiritual journey, David speaks of Jesus as the voice of a trusted friend: "gentle and powerful, always in solidarity with my soul; a deep current of identification and understanding." Through David's account of searching for and listening to this voice, he exemplifies how to face shame and acknowledge pain, so it can no longer dim the light within your soul. This book is not for the fainthearted who can't face their truth. It is a beacon of hope to all who don't want the pain of their past to determine their future path.

DR. RUTH ARMSTRONG | University of Cambridge, Cambridge, England

If we're honest, we all have a difficult story to tell, but few tell theirs better than David Zailer. In *Death of a Fisherman*, David speaks in clear, honest, self-revealing ways about how God wastes nothing in our lives, redeeming every abuse and loss and heartache. This compelling book will nourish the weary goodness inside you. There is courage, hope, and redemption on every page.

STAN BOYD, MD | ABEM

Death of a Fisherman should be required reading for every survivor of sexual assault, parental addiction, and abandonment. David's willingness to speak truth about his broken childhood, in light of profound, unspeakable trauma, demands that we not shirk from those who continue to suffer in silence!

CHAR FRENCH, NCACII, CSAC, CAADC, CCS, SAP | Outpatient Addiction Therapist, Addiction Clinical Supervisor, Interventionist

From page one, the quality of storytelling in *Death of a Fisherman*, and the wisdom told in simple perfunctory words, kept me reading more. David Zailer has done a masterful job of baring his soul in a way that makes us all yearn to be a bit more honest about ourselves. This brilliantly telling book has something to teach us all.

MICHAEL STONE, MD, ABAM, FASAM, FAAFP | Owner and Medical Director of Cornerstone of Southern California, Addiction Medicine Treatment Center

In *Death of a Fisherman*, David Zailer courageously invites us to journey with him as he recounts and reflects on the intermingled experiences of trauma, addiction, love, hope, and God that have shaped the journey of his life. This vivid, earthy, engaging account inspires us to not give up when life hurts but instead, often in sheer desperation, reach out to the God who has defeated the grave and continues to reach out to us. And it can inspire us to be the hands that reach out, on behalf of God, to others.

DR. STEPHEN TORR | Emmanuel Theological College, Chester, England

The moment I began reading *Death of a Fisherman*, I couldn't put it down. I felt I was right there in the story, looking into the lives of a family I understood and cared about deeply. David's authenticity and transparency transcends you to another place — a place where you can't help but be confronted with your own story of truth, suffering, and unforgiveness. Through David's words, you can envision the hand of God, moving and transforming from the inside out. A beautiful picture is created about how God can use the most damaging of experiences to create extraordinary transformation. David gently shows us all that running from the truth may be a daily temptation, but running into the hands of the One who loves you most is far more rewarding.

DIMETRA BARRIOS | Lead Pastor of Legacy Brooklyn Church, Brooklyn New York

In *Death of a Fisherman*, Zailer takes us through his transformation that happened not in spite of — but because of — the complicated family relationships he navigated during childhood. This book is for anyone who's been heartbroken by close personal relationships and needs a reminder that even in the darkest moments, healing and hope are already on their way.

SARAH THEBARGE | Author of *The Invisible Girls* and *WELL*

Written with incredible sensitivity and transparency, David Zailer shares his life story from stolen innocence to destruction, ruin to redemption. His words ring with hope for everyone with skeletons in their closet who is afraid to unlock the door. His journey is a must-read for all who need a "reset" button...and that's all of us!

DR. CURT DODD | Senior Pastor, Westside Church, Omaha, Nebraska

Honest stories well-told help us walk our own lives in truth. Real stories of embracing grace show us the way to grow in grace ourselves. David has told a story that is full of both grace and truth. We highly recommend it.

ALAN AND GEM FADLING | Founders of Unhurried Living, Authors of *What Does Your Soul Love?*

Death of a Fisherman is a powerful telling of grace and redemption. As David shares his story of ups, downs, and losses, there's one thing that is consistent: the presence and mercy of God to redeem him and all humanity. If you've suffered severe hurt and feel like there is no way out, this book will remind you that you're not alone and grace is accessible.

JEROME GAY JR. | Pastor of Vision Church, Raleigh, North Carolina, Author of *The Whitewashing of Christianity*

With clear, compelling writing, David Zailer shares his personal journey from a dysfunctional family in which the unholy trinity of trauma, religion, and addiction shaped his early life. Having kept it all hidden inside himself for many years, David describes the grief, anger, and loneliness this secrecy created. *Death of a Fisherman* is no Sunday school fairy tale. It's an inspiring story that is raw, real, and profoundly hopeful.

JIM HERRINGTON | Co-Founder of The Leader's Journey, and author of *The Leader's Journey: Accepting the Call to Personal and Congregational Transformation*

This strong and compelling memoir by David Zailer simultaneously treats the American family landscape with nostalgia and unflinching truth-telling. He paints the hearty masculinity of his childhood — with hot rods, fishing trips, front-yard football games, and boy-and-his-dog adventures — and makes us love and long for it. At the same time, he accurately describes the cruelty of the nominally Christian patriarchy and tells how it victimizes men and boys as well as women and girls. Courage is evident on every page, and David's humility and compassion are inspiring. At the end of the book, I could hear God's voice just as David did, my spiritual ears having been thoroughly washed of religious pretenses by his simple, honest prose.

AMANDA ANDERSON | Speaker and Author of *All My Friends Have Issues: Building Remarkable Relationships with Imperfect People (Like Me)*

The destructive power of shame hides in darkness and secrecy. The personal power to heal requires relational sunlight and fresh air. Like many good Southerners, David Zailer is an engaging storyteller. His narrative is sometimes raw but it is always honest. *Death of a Fisherman* is tenacious, heart-grabbing, and hope-filled storytelling of his commitment to journey away from darkness and toward the light. It is a story almost anyone can relate to. Read *Death of a Fisherman*, and be inspired to uncover the hidden shame in your life.

REVEREND DR. LAIRD BRIDGMAN, PsyD | Psychologist, Certified Employee Assistance Professional, Fellow, Academy of Cognitive and Behavioral Therapies, Assistant Professor, The Chicago School of Professional Psychology, Anaheim

Few ever return from the dark abyss of severe addiction and self-destruction. Fewer still can recount and tell of it with truthful courage, tender grace, and defiant hope. In *Death of a Fisherman*, David Zailer provokes a deep conversation about pain and grief, hope and faith. Those who are courageous enough to read *Fisherman* will find it to be a road map to navigate the often emotionally perilous inner journey where we will find the deepest freedom God has for us in Jesus Christ.

DR. KEN BAUGH | Executive Director for IDT Ministries, and author of *Unhindered Abundance: Restoring our Souls in a Fragmented Word*

I know of no one who more courageously confronts who he is and where he came from than David Zailer. Every page of this story had me rooting for little David to be allowed to be a normal boy, an impossibility given the deep pathology around him. How does one make sense of such dysfunction and find grace in it all? That was left for David to learn as an adult. In a story told with brutal honesty, David seeks truth and understanding, forgives what can be forgiven, and blesses what can be blessed.

REV. RONALD FELTMAN | Senior Pastor, Epiphany Lutheran Church, Elmhurst, Illinois

When I first read the title, *Death of a Fisherman*, I thought it sounded like something Hemingway might write. But *Fisherman* impacted me personally more than the last Hemingway book I read. David Zailer writes with a clear, descriptive style that carries you along throughout the story — and what a powerful story it is! You'll experience true hope and know that lasting life change is possible when you earnestly seek it. I applaud David Zailer for his courageous transparency in sharing his painful, arduous journey to a healthy life rich with forgiveness and grace.

RANDY MORAITIS, MA, CIP, BCPC, CADC II, ICADC | President, CarePossible, Inc.

Have you ever wondered if you can really change? In *Death of a Fisherman*, David Zailer lives out the anatomy of personal transformation. Holding nothing back, he dives into the relationships and life events that pushed him to the precipice of destruction and the long process of forgiveness that pulled him back. The details of David's life are his own, but the shape of his journey belongs to every one of us. It's the classic hero's journey. A rite of passage played out over a lifetime. Yes, we really can change. *Death of a Fisherman* shows us how personal transformation can be difficult and elusive, but always possible at the same time.

DAVID BRISBIN | Pastor, Counselor, Author of *The Fifth Way: A Western Journey to the Hebrew Heart of Jesus*

As I read *Death of a Fisherman*, I gained better insight into the good that God wants for us, even over the evil that has happened along the way. With stunning scenery, gut-wrenching rage, and hope-filled determination, this book will push your buttons. David Zailer uses deep, personal storytelling filled with love and challenge to pose direct, poignant questions that will impact the way you've seen your past and how you will see your future. Read this book, and perhaps even read it with a friend. The answer you long to know will appear.

TERRY LaDow, MS, CBPCC, LAADC, CLMC | New Perspectives Counseling

DEATH of a FISHERMAN

A Memoir of Family, Faith, and Forgiveness

DAVID ZAILER

This book is a memoir. It reflects the author's present recollections
of experiences over time. Some names and characteristics
have been changed, some events have been compressed,
and some dialogue has been recreated.

Hardcover: 979-8-218-08336-6
Paperback: 979-8-218-05700-8
E-book: 979-8-218-05699-5

Library of Congress Number: 2022915373

First paperback edition: November 2022

Edited by Joey O'Connor
Secondary Editing by Jessica Snell
Cover Art by Anne Goetze
Cover and Interior Layout by Natalie Lauren Design
Back Cover Photograph by Polly Haines Zailer
Project Management by Drew Tilton of Asio Creative
Special Thanks to Joan Tankersley of Five Key Collective

Published by
Homecoming Books
24040 Camino del Avion
Suite #E112
Dana Point, California 92629

In remembrance of Polly

Table of Contents

Preface

I WAS EIGHT YEARS OLD when I lost my Zebco rod and reel to the bottom of a lake north of Houston. That was also the day that the little fisherman inside of me died. It's taken a lifetime to bring him back to life.

This became especially clear a few years ago when an addiction treatment center in Houston hired me to help develop content for a series of educational videos. I traveled there four times over the next year to meet with others on the writing team. I was excited about the project because I enjoy writing. Writing for me is like finger-painting when I was a child. The process is messy and gets all over me, but I like the end result.

I am a born-and-bred Texan. I have lived most of my life away from The Great State, but I enjoy going back to visit when I can. Houston is filled with wildly diverse people full of old-school Texas warmth and charm. It is where I grew up and the memories are complicated, but even so, I wanted to go back and do the work.

I had no idea of the tests and the turmoil waiting for me there.

PRELUDE TO A JOURNEY

A FEW WEEKS BEFORE MY FIRST TRIP, I met a colleague for dinner after work. Carol and I get together once a year to renew our friendship and reconnect regarding our careers in the addiction recovery field. We always meet at the same Mexican restaurant in Los Angeles. As you walk in, the smell of warm tortilla chips lifts you by your nostrils and floats you to your seat on a rich aromatic cloud that seems to waft north from across the border. I always get there early to scarf down a basket of chips and salsa before she arrives.

There should be recovery meetings for chip eaters like me.

Carol was her usual radiant self. She's a rainstorm of delight moving through the noisy restaurant. Carefree and self-assured, she doesn't worry too much about what others might think. After giving me a quick hug, she slid into the brown leather booth across from me.

With mariachi music playing in the background, we ordered tamales with rice and beans, then chit chatted, catching up on life the way good friends do. Like the tiny broken chips at the bottom of the basket, we threw in tidbits of joking and gossip. I told her about my upcoming work in Houston, and I admit I was a bit smug. She smiled, then nodded and affirmed my talent just like I wanted her to. Carol has always been a great encourager, but she changed the direction of our conversation abruptly by squinting one eye and asking, "So David, what are *your* reasons for going to Houston?"

I thought this was a strange question, but without a moment's hesitation, I replied, "There are three things I want to do while there. I want to do good work on the videos. I want to deliver flowers to my mother's grave. I want to piss on my father's grave."

Carol instantly froze. She slowly set her fork down on her plate and stared at her food. It was as if she heard the ticking of a time bomb and was trying to determine its location. I cringed, wishing for a do-over to take my words back. She raised her head and sat tall in her seat, which made me sink lower in mine. She stared me straight in the eye but didn't say a word.

We sat in silence for a while as I pushed my food around on the plate. I think she wanted me to hear the message hidden within my words. Carol and I have known one another for over twenty years. She has witnessed time polish away much of my cantankerous character. Nevertheless, she clearly would not tolerate the way anger occasionally oozed out of me through crude comments. Certainly not while having tamales for dinner.

We said goodbye at the end of the evening with a warm hug and promised to get together again soon. Yet with busy schedules outweighing our best intentions, we both knew it would be another year before we met again.

My home was more than an hour away, so I found the closest freeway on-ramp, clicked on my favorite tunes, and settled into the flow. Traffic was light, and the weather was clear. My thoughts skipped from place to place. I felt thankful for how Carol gently expressed her deep care and concern without a word of criticism. Yet as I drove, I realized I was afraid of Carol knowing too much about me. She knew much of my story, but not all of it. I thought about how I hold back sometimes because I'm afraid of what others may think, even with those who love me the most.

That's when I noticed the music had begun to sound like fingernails on a chalkboard. I turned it off and drove in silence as the miles clicked by past Manhattan Beach, Long Beach, and into Orange County. I thought of Houston as I drove and the work waiting for me there. I was excited about the opportunity, but I also felt overmatched. I felt anxious about Houston and was afraid to face the music that played there.

FOR DECADES I KEPT a family photo album sitting on a shelf in my living room. It was a large, heavy book with a drab seventies-era, paisley-brown cover. My father didn't want it and passed it down to me after my mother died. I would pick it up on occasion, searching for happy memories. Each time I held it, I was always shocked by its bulk and weight. The irony of heavy memories is never lost on me.

In one photo after another, there I stand with my family. My father, Lew Zailer. My mother, Polly Haines Zailer. My sister, Debbie Zailer. And me. We pose and smile in many different settings, just like you see in every family album: family and school portraits, photos of extended family members, snapshots with neighbors, and vacation photos. Conflicted feelings of love and shame stir inside me whenever I look at these photos. Sometimes I've even felt sick to my stomach. For many years I've done my best to bury my family memories deep, orphaning them as dead and gone forever, but to no avail.

Shame hides within the pain of my family memories. It is a hungry jackal that sneaks back in the night to scavenge the rotting carcass of my forgotten soul.

As my first trip to Houston drew near, I decided to take another look inside the photo album. When I did, I immediately noticed how my family posed in the photos. We looked stiff, dated, and dusty, like unwanted window mannequins stored away and forgotten decades ago. Without thinking much of it, I peeled back the protective cellophane of the first page that kept the photos stuck on the sticky cardboard backing.

Dang, what am I doing? I asked myself.

For reasons I can't explain, exposing the photos to the fresh air felt good, like the first cool breeze of fall after a long hot summer. Mindful of how old and delicate they were, I carefully peeled each of them from the sticky cardboard. I handled them gently, as if they were newborn kittens, setting them on my kitchen table with great care. I removed every photo from the first page, and in so doing, I began to set my family memories free.

I paused for a moment and took a long look at the photos on the table. Suddenly, family history became very much alive in my mind, though fragile. Imagine newborn kittens mewing and wiggling in search of their mother's milk. I wanted to respond somehow, but there was no one there to help me. I was alone with all these photos. What was I to do with the burden of my memories?

All I could think was: *They deserved better, and so do I.*

I turned to the next page and did the same thing. Once again, it felt refreshing every time I removed a photo and set it on the table. I moved on to the third page and then to the next. Finally, every picture was freed from the album and staring up at me. Here we were, me and my family memories, as if gathered for breakfast together.

With the photos removed, I saw the old family photo album for what it was — heavy and empty!

I don't want to suffer this anymore, I thought.

I don't want this weight on my back any longer.

I took the empty photo album outside and threw it into the trash can.

I slammed the lid shut. *BAM!*

"Should have thrown that out years ago," I muttered as I walked back inside.

Back in the kitchen, I looked over the photos once more. Some were taken at the first family home where I grew up — a small, white house on the south side of Houston. I thought of this old house every time I had returned to Houston over the years. I wanted to drive by and see it but didn't know how to find it. However, with the photos no longer stuck to the album pages, they had more to say. My mother had written simple notes on the back of some of the photos with the date and place and short descriptions like "Debbie loves to feed the ducks," "David really likes puppies," and "Lew looks so handsome in his green shirt."

The notes she had written gave each photo a specific memory, most of which made me smile. Lo and behold, one of them had the address of the old white house on Glenlea

Street — a street name I then remembered — with a note asking that the photo be returned if a stranger ever found it. Finding this note from my mother felt like finding a hidden treasure. It showed the way to find my old house!

I was delighted with this discovery but I also felt conflicted. Since burying old memories is second nature to me, I did what was familiar. I scooped up all the photos, put them in a manila envelope, and set them on the side of my desk. That's the place where I put things I'm not ready to work on yet. Several days later, I picked the manila envelope up again and went back into the kitchen to lay the photos out on my kitchen table once more. I was more organized this time and laid the oldest first and the newest last to show a timeline of my family's life together. Looking at the photos, a hidden memory rose to the surface of my mind.

I was a boy of five or six, sitting in church next to my mother and sister. I was praying, asking God for a different home. I was pleading to go live with someone else.

As I scanned the photos more, my attention was drawn to my sister's face. Debbie was two years older than me. She was pretty, with copper-blonde hair and light-brown eyes. She always seemed more poised than most children her age, as if she had nothing to run or hide from. I stood beside her in most of the photos, doing my best to behave, but that was difficult for me. I was a rowdy, rambunctious boy with too much get-up-and-go. One photo shows Debbie and me at a petting zoo on a summer outing with our mother. I am standing behind her with crossed arms and an angry, scowling face, impatiently waiting my turn to pet the animals. It was obvious I wanted her out of the way. Big sisters lead the way for younger brothers, whether we admit it or not.

My mother was the photographer in our family. She often carried the hip camera of her day: a Kodak Instamatic. Snapping photos was one way she tried to hold us close, preserving and protecting her family the way good moms do. In almost every photo, she has her hand on my sister or me. Her hands exude warmth, always making a connection and giving us reassurance. I thought my mother looked pretty in the photos. She worked so hard to keep a smile on her face, always doing her best to make others feel at ease. I didn't understand it then, but it was her way of saving us from what was consuming her soul. Over the years, however, a deep furrow formed across her brow and cast a shadow over her beauty. The photos showed the pain in her face, which became more evident as time passed. My mother had the face of a woman suffering dark secrets that she kept to herself.

My father? He looks the same in all the photos. He has but one expression on his face. *Polite disinterest.*

Maybe he was hiding his embarrassment, as if tolerating us was the best he knew to do.

Polite disinterest?

In every photo?

Spread over all the years of our lives together?

Whatever my father's expression meant, he is not here now

for me to ask. If I could ask him, I doubt I would get a straight answer because straight answers were not how he handled life. My gut feeling was that my father simply did not want to be with us. He showed this to me in many ways over the years. You don't put memories like that into a family photo album.

MY MOTHER AND FATHER MARRIED in West Germany in 1955. He had been drafted into the U.S. Army and served there in a military office following World War II. They met just before his deployment, at a revival meeting where he played the piano and organ. He was something of a religious rock star back in the day and made a big impression on my mother. They got engaged by letter, and my mother traveled by ship to join him in Heidelberg, where my sister was born. After my father's military service, this young family of three returned and settled in Houston. My mother went to work as an executive secretary for an oil company. My father began teaching music in public school. He renewed his musical performance career by playing the organ at a big, popular church downtown.

I was born in Houston in 1958, two years after my sister. My parents carried me in a basket to church with them from my first week. When I was five, the church gave my mom my "Cradle Roll" that documented perfect Sunday School attendance since birth. Yes, we attended church as if our life depended on it, which it did because our family needed the paycheck my father earned for playing the organ.

We drove to church in my father's faded blue Chevrolet Biscayne. The floorboards in the back seat had rusted almost entirely away. As we drove down the freeway, I liked looking down through the holes to watch the pavement pass under my feet at sixty miles an hour. None of us thought it was a problem, so long as nobody outside our family knew about our rusty floorboards.

On the outside of the church hung a colossal neon sign as big as a car — JESUS SAVES! Inside, the auditorium was filled with plush, leather-cushioned seats with rounded seatbacks, varnished and polished to a high-gloss finish. (God forbid anyone might be uncomfortable in church.) Down front, there was a semicircular stage painted ivory white and trimmed with wood finished to match the seatbacks. The carpet was deep red, almost the color of blood.

Center stage sat a large pulpit, where the preacher laid his black leather Bible. He'd stand behind it in a dark three-piece suit, expounding about how God wanted to save all of us sinners and how God's blessings would go to those who were most obedient in turning from their sins. His weekly message was sure to preach the hell out of you.

Our church had the biggest choir in the city. The singers dressed in tailored white robes with a reversible stole made of satin worn at the neckline — red on one side, blue on the other. The choir director waved his arms with rhythmic command. Stage left stood a concert grand piano passionately played by a woman of outstanding talent. The pipe organ sat to the right and was played by my father with equal dedication and skill. It was a thrilling performance each week that made everyone applaud.

The church teaching gave me the impression that looking your best on Sunday was respectful and pleased God, so everyone wore their Sunday best. And you'd better never question "godly authority." "Strong believers" didn't doubt or ask questions. It seemed that those who wore the nicest clothes and showed the best faith pleased God the most. They would be the first in line to get his blessings. The rest of us would have to wait for spiritual leftovers.

The preacher spoke of the evils of this world and how we were all born as sinners condemned to hell for eternity — especially the drinkers and fornicators. I didn't know what drinkers and fornicators were, but I was glad I wasn't one of them. *At least not yet.* I never understood what I had done at such a young age to deserve eternity in hell. Apparently, just being born made me sinner enough. Thankfully, the preacher had a solution. Jesus was God's ready-made answer. Salvation free-of-charge. COME AND GET IT!

My mom, sister, and I sat in the same place every Sunday with mostly the same people every week. They sat with polite respect, appreciating the music and the preacher's words. I was bored and fidgety and passed the time scribbling pictures with the pencil and paper my mom kept in her purse to curb my rambunctiousness.

People flocked down the aisles at the end of every service to shake the preacher's hand and get their very own change-your-life-forever miracle. Men dressed in dark suits and women in pristine, colorful dresses that hung appropriately below the knee stood at the bottom of the stage. They were already sin-confessed and baptized saints, strategically positioned to embrace the newly arriving sinners and help them fill out white enrollment cards. Apparently, even Jesus didn't save sinners from the hell of paperwork.

I remember one Sunday when a lady ran down the aisle. She ran so fast that her flowery hat flew off and landed in the lap of the startled man who sat at the end of our row. Once it was her chance to confess, she told how she had been a slave to anger and beat her husband for drinking the whiskey she kept in her kitchen for medicinal purposes. Mom chuckled at that one. "Thanks be to God," she proclaimed, "no more hitting my husband. I'm going to be a new woman from today, and for all eternity."

A tall, handsome man in a suit and his blonde shapely wife in a red dress — seeing her made me sit up and pay attention — told how they had felt tortured for months because of their slothful disobedience. He liked to play golf on Sunday morning while she slept in. The Spirit had gripped them hard, and they had decided to "put an end to our selfish ways. You'll see us every Sunday from now until the day Jesus comes again."

The new converts testified about how bad they had been before and how, by leaving their seat and going down the aisle, they became transformed saints who would march with the rest of us forever into glory. I clapped my hands like crazy right along with everyone else for these miraculous displays of salvation.

Sunday School taught me how badly I needed Jesus to come live in my heart so that when I died, I would know beyond a shadow of a doubt that I was going to heaven, where the streets were paved with gold, instead of being burnt to a crisp in the flaming furnaces of hell for all eternity. Well, you can bet your bottom dollar I would've paid any price to escape the burning hell they said I deserved and get a free ride into heaven. Honestly though, I didn't give a bug's behind about how the heavenly streets were paved. Nevertheless, I was smart enough not to ask too many questions. I just smiled and tried to look my best, especially when next to someone who had nicer clothes than me.

After the service, my family and I would go to lunch with others from church and then return home to Glenlea Street, where I lived until I was six. Our house was no more than eight hundred square feet, with brick trim on the front. It was on the south side of town, a short distance from Hobby Airport. Planes took off over our house with a roaring thunder my father hated, but I loved. I played cowboys or soldiers or cops and robbers with other boys on the front lawn. Getting injured or wounded in battle was the best part. Why? Because a wonderful dark-haired girl my same age named Sofia, who lived across the street, came to my rescue and pretended to doctor my wounds. I'm sure Sofia was my first love.

I'll never forget the day her four-year-old brother was hit by a car two doors down from our house. As I played with other kids in a neighbor's yard, we heard a screech and a *thud*. Chaos exploded throughout the neighborhood. We ran toward the noise and saw our friend lying in the street. Blood was flowing from his head and trickling toward the gutter. The boy's father ran out of their house and picked up his son's broken body. He and another man rushed to a car while screaming at the rest of us to get back home. Tires screeching, they raced to the hospital, where our friend stayed for a very long time. He finally returned home, but he never played with us again due to the severity of his injuries.

I remember our first television set. My sister watched the Beatles and danced along in her white go-go boots. I liked to watch Westerns and dreamed of being a cowboy. I wanted to be one of the good guys who wore a white hat, a brown leather vest with a sheriff's badge, and a six-shooter I would only use with discretion and perfect aim. My father brought home an air conditioner one day and mounted it in the kitchen window. I would come inside after playing in the Houston sun and stand drenching myself in its cold wind.

My mother got us a dachshund my sister and I named Blacky. Blacky would find a way out of the backyard whenever he got the chance, making my father furious. He would chase Blacky around the neighborhood in his dress shirt and business slacks. Once he caught him, my father would beat poor Blacky with a rolled-up newspaper. My father cared more about how he dressed than how he treated my dog. He always dressed to make a dignified impression. His hair was always nicely combed, his shoes perfectly shined, his hands and fingernails impeccably manicured. He often reminded me that our family's well-being depended on the care and protection of his hands because of his profound musical responsibilities. I wonder if he thought about his hands when he was beating my dog.

Dark memories grip me as I tell the story of my father beating Blacky. The neighborhood Cub Scouts kicked me out because I was picking fights with other boys. I was also creating so many problems at school the principal gave my parents the names of doctors to sort me out. I remember seeing my mother and father argue in our small living room about all the trouble I was causing. He was shaking a rolled-up newspaper in my mom's face just like he did to Blacky. The yelling stopped when they saw me, but not before I heard him scream at her, "You're crazy and stupid!"

Then he turned to me and shook the paper in my face. "You don't need help! You need the kind of spanking you'll never forget!"

My father didn't tolerate Blacky for long. He gave him away to Mr. and Mrs. Hargis, who lived two doors down. Mr. Hargis was a short, wiry man of boundless energy who smelled of tobacco and a long day's work. Mrs. Hargis was a tall, willowy woman who nattered on and on to herself about who knows what. They were like Popeye and Olive Oyl to me, and they loved our little dog.

Mr. Hargis took me fishing when I was six. With my parents' permission, we left before sunrise wearing old shirts, blue jeans, and shoes we didn't worry about getting wet. He showed me how to bait the hook with a worm to hide the hook from view.

Wormy camouflage, I thought. *Mr. Hargis is a fishing genius!*

He gave me the chance to know the feeling of a fish tugging on the line and the experience of reeling it in to proudly take home. That same day, he also gave me a ride in his Jeep. A Jeep ride, for God's sake — ripping down a dirt road along the lake, we bounced around in the mud without seat belts. Mud flew everywhere and got all over us. We had no concern about what we looked like, how we smelled, or what little hurt might come our way. Mr. Hargis showed me God's great glory on that fish-catching, mud-filled day.

Fishing and Jeep rides aside, my neighborhood was not without scandal. A young unmarried pregnant woman moved in around the corner from our house. In the early 1960s, an unmarried pregnant woman in a mostly white south Houston neighborhood caused lots of whispers and raised eyebrows. My mom knew how to handle situations like this. She gathered possessions we didn't need and asked other ladies in the neighborhood to do the same.

Holding my hand, we crossed the street to meet the other ladies from the neighborhood. Kindness rising above scandal, my mom and the ladies walked to this woman's door as a group to deliver the items they had collected. Standing beside my mom at the pregnant woman's doorstep, I watched her look down and cover her face. Then she stopped, took in a deep breath, and smiled at my mom and the ladies. They all let out a deep sigh of relief.

She invited us into her front room; it was neat and tidy like Mom kept ours. Then she rushed to the kitchen and brought extra chairs. The ladies sat down to chat and drink iced tea with sugar and lemon wedges. I sat next to my mom, drinking grape Kool-Aid and feeling bored out of my mind. I noticed one of the ladies discreetly pull a small dark brown bottle from her purse and pour something into her tea. Mom looked at me as if to say, "Don't ask!"

I love this memory. It reminds me of who my mother really was. There were limits to my mother's kindness, but getting pregnant before being married wouldn't exclude you from them.

SUMMER RAGE

WHEN THAT DAY IN JULY ARRIVED for my first trip to Houston, I landed at Hobby Airport and made my way to the rental car counter. When I stepped outside to get the car, Houston's humidity slapped me in the face like it had an old score to settle against me. Once in the car, I cranked on the air conditioning and headed for my hotel on the west side of the city.

The next morning, I had a meeting at the recovery center to go over the video project. Afterward, I entered the address from my mother's note on the back of the picture into the rental car's GPS and began driving south toward my early childhood home. When I pulled off the freeway onto the surface streets, things began to look familiar. I even drove the last mile without help from the GPS.

I find it interesting how the patterns of life etch their way deep into our souls and then reemerge when we least expect it.

With one last turn onto Glenlea Street, I was halfway down the block when I saw my old white house on the left. Boy, did it look small. I pulled to the curb on the opposite side of the street and a couple of doors down. Right where Sofia's brother was hit by the car. I started to get out but then I stopped. I felt nervous and out of place. My old neighborhood didn't feel welcoming like I wanted it to. There was no threat or apparent danger, but it felt safer to stay in the car and view my childhood home from a distance.

I thought the old white house looked quite good considering its age. The paint was fresh, and the roof looked new. The front yard was dark green and recently mowed, with a tree in the middle that wasn't there when I was a boy. The owners had installed a small circular driveway to complement the even smaller driveway that led to a single-car garage. This tiny house had been well taken care of over the years, and I felt envious.

The front door and windows were wide open. Yellow curtains moved back and forth slowly in the hot midday breeze. I admired whoever lived there because living in Houston without air conditioning is tough to endure in the summer. I also noticed that cars were not parked on front lawns or set up on blocks around the neighborhood, as they often were when I lived there. Classier folk lived there now.

I saw an old woman slowly making her way in the direction of my old house. She carried a sack of groceries with her head down, looking only at the sidewalk. I felt her labored steps and slumped shoulders as if they were my own. As I watched her, I remembered things I wanted to keep forgotten.

I remembered walls of absence and isolation.

Rooms full of rejection and punishment.

A tiny house hemorrhaging with anger and shame.

As I remembered, the feelings flooded me, but then specific memories followed.

It's strange how the places we grow up in — the places that impact us most painfully — are often the first we forget, and the last we remember.

Among my painful memories were the nameless and mostly faceless women hired to stand in for my mother. She was diagnosed with clinical depression when I was about four. My father said nothing about it, but how do you explain clinical depression to a four-year-old? Thus, the stand-ins. All the women hired to care for my sister and me were good women. No doubt, every one of them was well-meaning, but none lasted for long. They all came and left the same way, riding the bus to our neighborhood in the morning and walking the last two blocks to our house, then doing it in reverse in the afternoon to go home. After they left, I would stay with the old lady who lived across the street. She had a nice wide lap to sit on and a small scruffy dog that would bite hard if I played too rough with it. I liked all the women who cared for my sister and me. I may have even adored them in a needy little boy kind of way because they seemed to have a heart for children like us whose mother wasn't there for them. Although as kind as they were, I always knew they were temporary and only just stand-ins until my mom came home. We all just did the best we knew how to do.

Sitting in the car looking at my old house, I remembered having so many questions until I was a teenager. That's when my father finally told me he had sent my mother to the Texas State Mental Hospital in Austin. Sent to the "loony-bin" against her will for electroshock therapy and other treatments common in that day. For all I knew, she had been strapped to a chair in a locked padded room on zombie drugs, hundreds of miles away from her home.

For reasons I couldn't understand at the time but would later emerge, my father's loyalty was to himself and to an image of himself that he loved and hid behind. He was self-obsessed and overwhelmed with frustration, unwilling and unable to love his wife simply as she was. She didn't satisfy his needs or expectations, so he sent her away as a hopeless and unwanted crazy woman.

Today I understand the complicated nature of my mother's diagnosis. I also know that there were options that my father could not or would not see. I believe she was sent away by someone more troubled than she ever was. His betrayal of her was a reflection of his rage.

Of course, at the time, I had no measure for my father's narcissism. He would reveal his true character to me in the coming years.

If you've ever been close to a narcissist, you'll know the dark sick feeling deep in your gut when people buy into the lovely charade the narcissist presents, while all they can see is that something is wrong with you.

As children, and sometimes even as adults, we absorb sick feelings from others because we're not mature enough to face them and set boundaries. Then as we grow older, we bury them deep for our sense of safety.

Cemeteries are often places filled with such memories and emotions. It was time for me to go to the place where my parents were buried and face what I needed to face.

As I drove away from Glenlea Street, a quiet voice inside me said, *Mom never got enough flowers.*

I saw an H-E-B supermarket and pulled in, knowing the store would have flowers for sale. It was cool inside and bustling with people. Announcements on the public address system were so loud it hurt my ears. I quickly found the flower kiosk and looked over the colorful options before selecting a bouquet of red roses.

Just as I arrived at the shortest checkout line, a woman wearing a Houston Texans T-shirt cut me off and scooted ahead of me. Her cart was filled with enough food to feed a football team for an entire season. Because I only had flowers to buy, I thought she might let me go first, so I moved forward a step but no such luck. She blocked me out.

The cashier wore a sparkly smile and seemed to genuinely enjoy interacting with her customers. She processed the groceries with the efficiency of a Ford truck assembly line. She and the woman ahead of me bantered about raising teenagers and being busy moms. She took each item one after the other, scanned it, and then passed it along to a bored-looking young man who bagged it all up. *Beep! Beep! Beep!* One barcode after another. I could see this would take a while as the line grew longer behind me. When the woman ahead finally pushed her truckload of groceries on, the cashier turned to me with a big smile and said, "Wow, look at those roses! You must be in trouble with a woman. What're you making up for?"

Her humor struck a nerve, and I angrily snapped back, "Just ring me up!"

I followed that with words I should never use but sometimes do anyway when I'm not careful. My bad words shocked the others who were in line with me. The man directly behind me looked at me like I had horns on my head and a forked tail on my backside. The woman behind him scowled at me as if she wanted to stuff a bar of soap in my mouth and rinse it with a firehose. I looked back at the cashier, who started to giggle, but she caught herself, and then she smiled like she enjoyed seeing me get fed a piece of humble pie. As I handed her a twenty-dollar bill, I leaned toward her and quietly apologized for my outburst. She leaned back toward me as she counted the change back into my hand and said with a smile, "I hope the rest of your day goes better."

My heart quickened as I drove toward the cemetery. I felt terribly late for something important. Thirty years late! I have missed my mother every day since her death in 1986, but I was only now coming to revisit her resting place. I wanted to honor her, but I did not want to be near my father, who was buried beside her. I despised him for the hurt he inflicted upon my mother, and yet I sensed he was the real reason I had come this far. I hated but couldn't deny that I loved one parent while harboring decades of rage against the other.

I drove into the cemetery through a wrought-iron archway and gate that connected stone walls on both sides. To find the exact spot where they were buried, I stopped at the office for directions, but once I left there, I found my way from memory, just like when driving to the house on Glenlea Street. Thousands had been laid to rest there, with row after row of headstones and markers. Some had flowers on them; others had motionless American flags waiting for a breeze to come and bring them to life. The grass was pale green with brown spots here and there. The trees were in full bloom. The air was heavy and hot.

I parked in the exact spot where I stood and said a final goodbye on the day when Mom was laid to rest. I sat for a few minutes with the car off, remembering how well-composed I was leading up to that day. At twenty-seven, most people thought I was tough as nails. Some people even said that I was mean and calloused — and I won't argue that. No matter how tough I appeared to be, I became completely undone the day Mom was buried. I was overcome with the grief of her life and that of my own. She was here one day but dead the next. Dead in the most tragic of ways. It was so unexpected that I never got to say goodbye or tell her how much she meant to me one last time. I'd spent the three days before her memorial caring for my father and sister the best I knew how. I managed funeral plans and coordinated travel with extended family. My mom's brothers came from Colorado with their wives, and her sister came with her husband from Tennessee. I answered most of the phone calls, offering polite answers to nosey people. I stayed busy doing things for my family because that is what I always did when Mom was not there to do it for us.

Before the gravesite service, there was a memorial service at the church where my father played the organ. This church wasn't the same church where he played when I was a small boy. About ten years before Mom's death, he left the former church to play at this new one. Ever supportive, Mom went with him every Sunday morning and evening, often sitting alone. Instead of sitting next to her once he'd finished playing, like the pianist who sat with his wife, my father chose to stay seated at the organ, leaving her to sit by herself. She was not unpopular, though. Her memorial service was packed with friends from both churches who came to pay their respects. After the service at the church, family and a few close friends gathered at the graveside. Everyone was somber and respectful as they stood circled around her grave. The preacher was calm and dignified in his delivery. The formality of his words felt cold to me. They pelted against my heart like sleet falls from the sky in winter.

I was the last one to leave the graveside. One by one, I thanked everyone for being there as they walked to their cars to go. Once the last car drove away, I took a moment for a last look back. As I saw my mother's casket sitting there alone, I thought of her sitting by herself in church all those years and realized that was how her life ended — alone! My composure ran out, and I collapsed on the front seat of the car and sobbed like never before. It was like drowning.

I heard a car drive by where I was parked. My mind returned to the present. I opened the car door, stepped out, and began walking toward my parents' gravestone. I moved carefully, watching every step as if there might be a snake in the grass, ready to bite. As I approached their headstone, I saw my mother's name: Polly H. Zailer. My father's name was to the left of hers on the marker, but I ignored it and kept my gaze fixed on hers.

A good name, I thought. Just saying *Polly* to myself brought comfort.

"Hello," I said out loud. "I'm sorry for being gone for so long."

I felt embarrassed and ashamed for being away all those years and placed the roses on the grass next to the headstone on my mother's side but then repositioned them to cover my father's name on the marker. This time was only for her.

"You deserved so much better," I said out loud.

I've said this to her in my mind at least a thousand times before. Then, without thinking, I laid down on the grass with my head next to her side of the headstone to be as close as possible to her.

Pain and loss can make you do things that look strange in the eyes of others. At that moment, looking strange to someone else was of no concern to me. It was the best I had to give to her.

THE GRASS IN HOUSTON can feel rough against your skin. I remembered how it rubbed a rash when roughhousing on it when I was a boy. I've always liked the way it smells when it's first cut, like fresh hay inside of an old barn. It feels hot to the touch in the afternoon summer sun. Yet, there's often muddy wetness just underneath the surface from the rain and humidity.

I had spent that morning in office meetings at the recovery center, working on the video content with the team. Now I was lying on the grass in a cemetery baking in the hot sun with muddy moisture soaking into my shirt and trousers. It didn't bother me.

My father bothered me, though. Even though he was dead, I resented him for being there. I thought of digging up his rotten remains and hauling them to a landfill, but that wasn't going to happen. I tried my best to ignore his presence. Yet it seemed like he was listening with his ear to a door that I had worked hard to keep closed and locked. This reunion with Mom felt good. I didn't want him here but he was here, inescapable and untouchable! What could I do about it?

I thought of pissing on his grave. I stood and looked around to see if I could get away with it, but others visiting their loved ones were within eyesight. Several men were digging with a backhoe a hundred yards away. And Mom was here. Humiliating my father, or myself, would be the last thing she would want me to do. She always loved us both.

I realized I was standing in the small space between their graves. Irony emerged: I've been stuck between my parents most of my life. Stuck wanting to honor my mother for her love and exposing what was hidden behind my father's well-manicured image. To the right was my mother, and how I was powerless to care for her. On the left was my father, who ignored anything that didn't interest him — including me.

To help explain, I'll tell you more about my relationship with my father. In the hope of making things better between us, in 2001 I challenged him to face the brutal impact his lies and deceptions inflicted on our family. He would have none of it. That is when the long silence between us began. When he died in 2015, I would not have known had not my long-lost cousin Bryan kindly reached out to tell me of his death. Bryan was from my father's side of the family. We had not seen one another or spoken in twenty-five years.

I had always wanted to be a good son. Like any child, I wanted my father's approval. I yearned for his attention and acceptance. As a teenager, I desperately needed him to be someone I could respect, but he failed to live in a way that made it possible to respect him. Yet even after all these years, I cannot turn my heart away from him. God knows how hard

I've tried. My father has been a cold, dark shadow that has followed me wherever I have gone.

My father's public image was his firstborn — his chosen heir, you could say. He was a handsome man. A little taller than average with sandy-brown hair and hazel-green eyes. He had a pleasant personality and immense musical talent that he showed off whenever he got the chance. People were drawn to him. They loved him for his talent. My mom, my sister, and I loved him simply because he was ours. We would do anything for him, but we were mostly his stage props. He stood in front of us when we made him look good. Or he would hide behind us when he needed to, using our shortcomings to hide his own. My father's secrets were his most protected possessions. We were the keepers and guardians of his secrets.

As I stood there between my parents' graves, I heard someone call out, "Excuse me! Excuse me! Are you all right, sir? Is there anything I can do for you?"

I looked in the direction the voice came from and saw a man about sixty feet away walking toward me. It was one of the men digging with the backhoe. He was a decent-looking fellow, at least twenty years younger than me. African American with a neatly trimmed beard and his head shaved smooth. He wore a maintenance uniform, muddy from the waist down and soaked with sweat — a mark of toil and labor that I know well. I laughed silently to myself. *A gravedigger has come to rescue me!*

I shouldn't have been surprised, I guess. What sane person lies on the hot grass wearing business clothes when it's a hundred degrees? In a cemetery, no less?

He kept walking toward me, so I took a few steps toward him, wanting to meet him halfway and end the conversation as quickly as possible.

"Thank you," I said. "But no thank you."

Something about him reminded me of myself when I was younger. I spent years working long days in the heat. Often finishing the day's work well after dark by stripping down to my birthday suit in the garage because my clothes were too sweaty and muddy to take inside. Because of the hard, dirty work I grew up doing, I admire those who bust their knuckles to make their way. It's a way of life I know well and respect. This young man seemed to embrace his labor and toil with integrity.

He stopped about fifteen feet away and stood there looking at me. I kept looking back at him, not knowing what else I was supposed to say. I was in my sixties, and my work was helping others, but now, someone many years younger than me — a gravedigger no less — was there offering to help me. It was a standoff of sorts. There was nothing comfortable about it!

Accepting help is God-awful hard sometimes.

To relieve the inner tension I felt, I thought, *Jesus! At least he's not come to bury me yet!*

After a few more moments, he finally gave an assertive nod and turned to walk away. I went back to stand between my parents' graves and stayed there for well over an hour, just thinking. My back grew stiff. My feet began to ache. The pain magnified the growing fatigue in my soul. I noticed that my shirt was soaked sweaty and my pants were caked with dried mud. *I must look like a gravedigger in a starched button-down shirt.* I chuckled to myself.

I wasn't ready to leave, so I stood there longer still.

Thirty minutes later, the young man came back again. He approached from a different direction this time, almost like he was sneaking up on me.

"Is there anything I can do for you?" he said, repeating his question from before.

He carried a bottle of water with him this time and held it out, offering it for me to take. I felt more comfortable with him this time, but I politely thanked him nonetheless and declined the water. God forbid I might look needy or weak, but he wasn't someone who gave up easily and he continued to stare at me, longer this time than the first time. With an even more insistent look, he said, "I'm around here until dark if you need anything."

Then he turned and walked away once more.

I noticed a bench under the shade of an oak tree about forty feet away and cussed my stupidity for not seeing it sooner. I walked over and sat under the tree. Then I put my elbows on my knees with my head down and stared at the grass.

I thought of how trees are in their fullest bloom during seasons when we need their shade the most, and I was grateful for the tree. The late afternoon sunlight flickered through the limbs and leaves. It cast shadows on the ground at my feet. Light and dark images in contrast showed how the tree moved in the wind. It was simple beauty to behold. Neither light nor dark gave way to the other. Side by side together, they revealed natural shape and distinction. I didn't notice the beauty in just the sunlight or in just the dark, but when I noticed how they fit together, highlighting one another, the beauty was easy to see.

I sat there for another half an hour, watching the shadows move back and forth on the ground. I thought of others who'd sat under this tree. People who shared similar experiences of loss and sadness, and perhaps even anger like me.

Loss and sadness harden into rage when I keep it to myself. Yet when I thought of others who'd sat under this tree, I suddenly didn't feel so alone. Then I heard the snap of a twig behind me and turned to look.

My friend the gravedigger had slipped up on me from behind. He didn't hesitate this time. With a bloody-knuckled hand, he set the bottle of water down beside me on the bench, looked me straight in the eye, and said, "It's awful hot out here. You need to have some water."

With that, he turned and walked away.

Once he had left, I picked the bottle of water up, twisted off the cap, and brought it to my lips. Once the water flowed into me, I realized how deep my thirst had been.

I HAD PLANNED TO RETURN TO WORK but had stayed at my parents' gravesite longer than I anticipated. So I decided instead to go back to my hotel, a short fifteen-minute drive away. As I passed through the revolving doors, I saw my reflection in the glass and how dirty my clothes were.

"Have car trouble, sir?" asked the young lady at the concierge's desk as I walked by.

"Nope! I'm good," I replied.

I gave her a thumbs-up and walked onto the elevator as fast as I could.

Once in my room, I kicked off my shoes and slumped into a chair. A half hour or so later, I showered and dressed and went back downstairs to the hotel restaurant. I hadn't eaten since breakfast and was starving, so I ordered a steak and baked potato — loaded of course. As I waited for dinner, I tried to enjoy an Astros game on a TV mounted high on the wall, but I couldn't stop thinking about the cemetery. I couldn't ignore my hurt and anger or deny how much I cared about my father.

I must admit what I'm sure you already know. I've been writing about my father as if holding a knife to his throat. I've held on to my desire for vengeance, trying to hold him accountable and make things turn out the way I want them to be, even though he is long dead and gone.

It's so much easier to inflict pain on others than face it for ourselves.

I looked forward to putting the day behind me and getting a good night's sleep. As I rode the elevator back to my room after dinner, questions echoed in my mind.

Are you willing to explore dangerous territory?

Will you honestly face your rage?

While preparing for bed, I decided to revisit my parents' gravesite again because I still had three more days of work at the recovery center. I didn't want to deal with the afternoon heat again, so I got up at 4:30 a.m. to start each of those mornings with a jog. Jogging is good for my body and especially good for my head. After my run each morning, I showered and grabbed breakfast at the hotel, then swung by the store to get flowers for my mother, and arrived at the cemetery easily before 7 a.m.

The morning cool was perfect, with dew still on the grass. The stillness and quiet made the grounds feel comfortable and private. For the next three mornings, I spent that time standing at my parents' headstone or sitting on the bench under the oak tree, listening to the birds sing. I kept telling myself that it was okay to remember the ugly parts of my life but be careful not to get lost in them. This helped me relax and be there with *both* of my parents.

Hurt and love together — without the need to choose sides.

On the last morning, as I was about to leave the cemetery for work, a white pickup drove by, then circled back and parked two spaces from where I was parked. My friend the gravedigger was behind the wheel. I saw he was rolling down his window, and so I walked over and immediately thanked him for the kindness he showed a few days earlier. He smiled and nodded, then we chatted about the beauty of the morning and my return home to California later that day. He winked and said, "And we're not muddy yet!"

With that, we both threw our heads back and laughed like it was the funniest joke ever.

Then, without thinking, I held up my smartphone and asked, "Would you take a selfie with me?"

"Sure, I'd be happy to," he replied.

He stepped out of his truck and walked over to stand beside me. His shirt was embroidered with the name Andrew.

"My name is David," I said, and stuck out my hand.

"Andrew," he responded as he reached back to shake it.

Then we each put an arm around the other's shoulder. I raised my phone — *Click!*

With the sound of the click, I remembered how my mother loved taking photos. She knew that any memory, even the ugly ones, might become a treasure someday if it's not forgotten and lost.

Andrew and I talked a bit more and then concluded our chat by shaking hands once more. As Andrew got back into his truck, he said, "Glad to see you're doing so well this morning."

He started his truck. I started my rental car. Off we went to work.

Later that evening, I drove to the airport but made a short detour to Glenlea Street and took a picture of my old house. Knowing exactly where to find it made me feel good and grounded. Like using a map to find your way begins with finding *your place* on the map.

Once on the plane, I relaxed in a window seat as we took off and climbed to cruising altitude. I thought of meeting Andrew and looked at our selfie. Andrew works humbly as a gravedigger, work that some may think is dirty or unclean, but I think of it differently. From the years I worked in construction, I know how such work requires skill and thoughtful precision. It is a kind and sacred service for the dead *and* the living.

I sat in silence during the flight, sipping water and eating the free almonds one by one. I gazed out the window as the terrain of West Texas, New Mexico, Arizona, and Southern California passed beneath me. The American Southwest has intrigued me ever since I was a boy. I dreamed of being there while I watched *Gunsmoke, Bonanza,* and John Wayne Westerns. Over the past twenty years, I've explored tens of thousands of miles of that wilderness by motorcycle. It's not what I do in the desert that is so important, but what happens to me when I am there.

I landed after dark and grabbed a taxi for home. As I sat in the back seat, I remembered looking through the holes in the rusty floorboards of my father's Chevrolet. A picture from the family album came to mind — a grainy black-and-white of my father when he was eleven or twelve.

That night before bed, I printed the photo of Andrew and me and pinned it to my office wall to remind me of the persistent kindness given me even before I understood how much I needed it. I then pulled out the photo of my eleven-year-old father from the manila envelope. He was standing with his father and mother and sister and brother. I noticed he was wearing his Boy Scout uniform. The shame of being kicked out of Cub Scouts hit me hard when I compared his experience to mine.

Why did this picture come to mind?

I didn't know the answer, but I did know that it's impossible to appreciate the value in something when it's kept hidden out of sight.

I pinned my father's picture on the wall next to Andrew and me. Perhaps it could help me better understand my father's life, and my own life as well?

I DID CHORES AROUND THE HOUSE that weekend and ate too much. Monday rolled around, and I was fresh and ready for the week. When working at my desk, I occasionally looked at the photo of my father and his family. His Boy Scout uniform was impeccable. The scarf was knotted exactly right and hung perfectly centered down his chest. His mother stood behind him with her hands placed on his shoulders like she was posing him on display. He was smiling, but his eyes were shut. The old "say cheese," then blink routine. Yet even with his eyes closed, I felt like he was looking back at me.

I thought back to when I stood facing him after being kicked out of Cub Scouts. As I mentioned earlier, they kicked me out for picking fights with other boys, which was true, but there was more to the story. They also caught me peeking underneath our den mother's skirt. That's why they kicked me out for good! I can still see my father standing there red-faced with a wooden paddle from his college fraternity in his hand. He was about ready to use it on me when Mom yelled, "Stop it! Can't you see he's feeling bad enough already!"

Our memories never leave us. They rush back and forth inside of us like deeply hidden currents.

Weeks later, I stopped work for a moment to look at my father's picture and the one of Andrew and me and noticed *where* I had placed them: directly underneath a bronze rubbing of the Virgin Mary and baby Jesus. My father had made this beautiful rubbing several decades before, etching the images onto black cloth from the carved-stone floor of a Catholic church in Europe. He knew how much I liked it and sent it to me a few years after my mother died. I framed it and hung it on my wall, where it has stayed all these years. However, once my father and I stopped talking, I stopped noticing it was there. Its beauty was forgotten, even though it hung in plain sight.

I then pictured my father down on his hands and knees, working hard to make this exquisite rubbing. He could not have made it without getting his hands dirty. Even when I was a boy, I saw how hard he worked for what he loved and I felt jealous. My father gave his music and artwork more time and attention than he did to me when I was a boy and needed it most.

THE SECOND TRIP TO HOUSTON was on my calendar for the fall. I felt an intense, persistent urgency to revisit my parents' gravesite again while I was there. Before I went, I wanted to know more about my father and how he grew up. I contacted relatives from his side of the family and asked them what they could tell me. I also looked over the small number of family documents I had received along with the family photo album. This was some of what I learned.

My father was born in 1931 to George and Vesta Zailer in McCook, Nebraska. He was a middle child with an older sister and a younger brother. George and Vesta moved their family to Denver in the early 1940s and bought a duplex. George died young, at age forty-six, when my father was nineteen. My father never said a word to me about him, but from relatives, I learned that George was a friendly, popular man at church on Sundays but hard to get along with everywhere else. He worked as an armed guard who protected bank shipments for the railroad, and he knew violence firsthand. I was told that he carried his .45-caliber semiautomatic everywhere he went. I bet he did!

George was also known to be terribly harsh with his wife and children. From what I was told, my father got the worst of it. George took them on Sunday drives through the mountains west of Denver and used the day to tease and ridicule my father. After stopping for food or restroom breaks, George hustled everyone back into the car but slammed the car door in my father's face. George sped away, leaving my father by the side of the road with dust and gravel spraying him in the face. They would return hours later to find my father sitting alone, bawling his eyes out. George thought it was hilarious fun. Vesta ignored the harm it was doing to her son.

I remember Vesta from when I was a small boy. I called her Grandma Vesta to her face, but I never thought of her as a grandmother. She was distant and coldhearted. No matter what I called her, she was just Vesta to me.

Vesta was short and stout — a human teapot without the spout. Her simple dresses were hemmed at mid-calf and hung like potato sacks. She wore nylon stockings that stopped just above her knees. I remember when the wind would catch her dress, she would gyrate like a drunken monkey to keep it from flying up and showing any skin of her leg. I'd giggle at the sight of it. Mom would shush me. Strange to think about it now, but I also remember Vesta's shoes. They were black leather lace-ups with wing-tip trim and semi-pointed toes with three-inch heels. A fashionable mix of army boots and high heels that she kept polished to perfection.

Sunday church was the most important thing in Vesta's life. She was there whenever the doors were open, but not necessarily with George. They often argued about where to attend, so they would go to different churches. Yet the disagreements with George never dimmed Vesta's religious dedication; she carried her Bible everywhere. Scripture verses rolled off her tongue with assumed authority, and she hummed hymns most every waking moment. She was a high-heeled, army-booted, hymn-chirping songbird.

Vesta inspired my father's inborn musical talent when she bought a piano for the family, and he took to it with passion. She considered him a musical prodigy and began investing in piano lessons for him when he was five. It paid off. By nine years old, my father played the piano at her church every week. He received rave reviews from the worshippers, which of course thrilled Vesta to no end. I'm sure this is where my father learned how to be musical royalty at church.

Vesta remarried after George died and lost his pension as a result. When her second husband died four years later, his life insurance went to his children from his first marriage. Her only source of support was the rent from the tenants who lived next door in the duplex. Vesta needed more income and was lonely. For companionship and to make ends meet, she rented out a room to a woman named Lois.

WHEN I WAS ABOUT SIX, my father took our family to Denver to visit Vesta one summer. The steps leading up to the front porch were almost as wide as the duplex itself. On the porch were two doors — one to each side of the duplex.

During our visit, I made up a game where I would run up the steps hooting and hollering, then slide down the handrails. Running up, I pretended I was a cowboy. On the slide down, I was an Indian. To no one's surprise, my game was a big nuisance to the family who lived next door. Vesta scolded me often for making such a commotion. My father told me repeatedly a good boy is to be seen but never heard. I'm sure I heard this at least a thousand times before I was eleven. Mom pleaded with me to be polite and quiet; she always wanted to keep the peace. Lois, Vesta's renter, said I was cute! She didn't give a rip about the noise I made or the family who lived next door.

Lois was a large woman. I bet she outweighed my father by fifty pounds. Her hair was jet-black. She kept it oiled and combed like Elvis Presley. She wore denim jeans with cuffs folded up at the bottom, black boots, and a black leather belt that matched her boots. In her Western-style shirts with pockets that snapped, she kept her cigarettes and a Zippo lighter.

Lois drove a truck for a living and took me with her one day to work. Mom threw a fit when we got home that evening because Lois never had permission to take me, leaving Mom sick with worry all day long. The next day, Lois brought me a gift. It was a box of fifty plastic army men! Each figure triggered my boyhood imagination. They shot rifles! Launched bazookas! Fired machine guns! A make-believe army, where I was in command!

Lois dominated life at the duplex. Mom was the only one bothered by this. Lois made troubling comments to her when no one was around to hear except for me. I never understood what they meant.

One day when my father wasn't around, I watched as Lois crept up on my mother while she was hanging wet laundry on the line to dry. Lois grabbed her bottom and reached to grab her breasts. Mom jumped like a deer wounded by a rifle shot. Her face washed pale with shock and fear. Lois laughed and went after her again, but my mother turned and ran for the back door. She slammed it shut and locked it behind her. *Bam! Clunk!*

When I saw what had just happened, I first froze, then I burst into tears. Lois looked in my direction, saw me crying, and snorted, "Humph!"

Mom locked herself in her room upstairs until my father returned. When he did return, she ran to him and told him what happened. After that, she went to Vesta, told her every thing, and then back to my father again. Lois denied it all. My father and his mother just stood there. They both dismissed her plea for help with shrugged shoulders. Vesta went back to humming her hymns. My father called my mom crazy. He told me later, "Your mother was seeing things. Again!"

From what he said, I must have been seeing things too.

About a week later, Mom was washing dishes, and Lois crept up behind her once again. She tried to kiss her! Mom threw back her head and screamed. As she broke away from Lois's grasp and ran out of the kitchen, she dropped a plate on the floor that shattered to pieces. Just like before, Mom ran to my father, who was outside talking with the neighbors. He refused to believe her again! Desperate, she ran upstairs to Vesta, who was napping. Vesta didn't believe her either. And once more, Lois laughed and denied doing anything wrong. This time though, Vesta and my father did react. Vesta flashed red hot with anger over the broken plate and began screaming at my mother, accusing her of lying to avoid blame for breaking the plate. After tearing into my mother, just like before, Vesta went back to humming her hymns, not bothered by anything. My father's face turned purple in anger and stayed that way for hours. Mom went upstairs to the bedroom and didn't come out again until the morning.

Sometimes late at night, I would get out of bed when I thought everyone was asleep to play army in the upstairs hallway. There, I would see Lois sneak in and out of Vesta's bedroom in the dark. When she saw me, she bent down close with her finger to her lips and said, "Shhhhh, don't you just love your army men?"

That summer, I watched my mother wither. Her hands started trembling. Her foot began wiggling up and down when she sat with one leg crossed over the other. Her eyes grew fixed and squinted as if she were always staring at a bright piercing light. She anxiously paced back and forth across the room, wringing her hands.

As I reflect on those experiences, I don't think the assaults Lois inflicted on my mother are what damaged her most. I believe what was most hurtful was my father's refusal to stand up and defend her. For years afterward, I listened to my parents argue about what happened back at Vesta's. You couldn't consider them real arguments. Mom pleaded for my father to believe her. She begged for understanding and protection, but he wouldn't listen. Instead, he kept coming at her with, "You're sick! You're crazy! You're hallucinating!"

Over time, my father's cruel words grew on my mother like a disease.

His words made him a hard man to forgive.

My FATHER TOOK A NEW JOB teaching music at a university the same year we visited Vesta at her duplex. He had long dreamed of being a tenured college professor, and this was his next big step to make it happen. Before you could say *box it all up*, movers had our belongings loaded into a truck and delivered to our new house across town, near the university. It was more than twice the size of our old house and built entirely of brick. "Absolutely hurricane-proof," my father said with pride.

It had a two-car garage, a living room with connecting dining room, a den with yellow-orange shag carpeting, and wood-grain paneling. Mom was thrilled to the moon with her new kitchen, except for the floor. It was black and white tile laid in a checkerboard pattern. She scrunched up her nose when she looked at it and had it replaced as soon as we could afford it. The kitchen cabinets were coffee-colored brown, and the countertops lime-green Formica. The electric stove and oven made her smile as big as I ever saw. "I can cook a turkey in this thing," she exclaimed. "It even has a broiler!"

My parents' bedroom at the back of the house was big enough for a queen-sized bed, two dresser drawers, and my mother's sewing table. It had a walk-in closet and a bathroom.

My sister's room was at the front of the house. She hung up posters of Bobby Sherman, the Monkees, and pictures of kittens. When she was a teenager, she got a waterbed and spent hours floating on it while listening to Joni Mitchell, James Taylor, or Crosby, Stills & Nash on her record player, while incense burned on her nightstand.

My room was in the middle of the house and shared a wall with my parents' bedroom. I put up pictures of cowboys and horses but later changed them to posters of my favorite baseball and football teams. Through the wall shared with my parents' room, I could hear their muffled voices when they talked late at night and sometimes other sounds that made me cower under the covers in fear. As a boy, I couldn't identify exactly what those sounds were, but I know they were not the sounds of a young husband and wife sharing passion and pleasure. They were the sounds of punishment and pain, followed by stifled whimpers of humiliation and shame.

What I liked best about our new house was the automatic central air-conditioning. It was technical wizardry that had to come straight from NASA! Who else could come up with such a wonder? The condenser sat just outside my window and made a loud *ka-clank* noise when it started a cooling cycle before settling into a steady hum. That noise startled me awake at night for weeks after we moved in. I'd jump out of bed thinking that something was breaking through my window. *Ka-clank!* In time, that terrible noise became a comfort, letting me know that cool air was on the way and the hum would drown out the frightening sounds coming through the other side of the wall.

Nevertheless, my father's new job and our new house made us all excited for the future. Mom rebounded from her experiences at Vesta's duplex and looked forward to having company over for dinner in our dining room. She wanted to invite people from church to play board games, with punch and cookies in the den. One afternoon, she came home to discover my father had moved a piano and an electric organ into the dining room area without discussing it with her first. "I'm going to make extra money giving lessons," he announced.

Mom cried when she saw what he had done. To make up for her disappointment, my father bought a new refrigerator, which made her happy. The freezer in the old fridge had to be defrosted every two weeks. Mom hacked away at the ice to get the frozen meat to thaw and cook for supper. It even made her cuss sometimes. She'd yell, "Darn! Darn! Darn!"

When it came to cussing, Mom was a lightweight.

My father's new job and salary provided new things for all of us. Mom was able to buy new dresses and shoes. She started to collect simple costume jewelry that she kept in a small box on her dresser. My sister also received dresses, shoes, but more importantly, new records. I was given a bicycle with a banana seat and high-rise bars.

Mom was a whizbang with S & H Green Stamps from the grocery store, redeeming them for extra luxuries for us all. I got a football, a junior-sized catcher's mitt, a Louisville Slugger, and a Zebco rod-and-reel.

My Zebco was the finest setup any seven-year-old fisherman could dream of owning.

One day my father came home with a brand-spanking-new Ford Mustang — a slick and shiny two-door coupe with yellow paint and black vinyl interior, automatic transmission, and an AM radio.

"No more rusted-out floorboards," my father exclaimed. "I got under-coating!"

While a Mustang was one of the coolest cars you could buy in 1965, Mustangs were never a family car. The back seat was smaller than small. The rear windows were the size and shape of a pizza slice. On scorching Houston days, my sister and I baked like potatoes riding in the back seat. Nevertheless, I applauded my father for the new car. Celebrating him and his accomplishments was how I worked to keep him happy with me.

OUR NEW HOUSE sat in the middle of the block on Sandpiper Street. It was one of the hundreds of similar homes in a neighborhood the size of a small town. It had a nice front and back yard with the same scratchy grass I had laid on next to my mother's grave. There was a beautiful tree in the front yard that my father absolutely loved. When I was ten, I inflicted a gaping wound on the side of it, leaving a scar in the bark that would last for years to come. Mom enrolled my sister and me in Sutton Elementary School, just two blocks away. My sister was in third grade, and I was in first. I rode my bike everywhere and learned every street in the neighborhood. I discovered the best places for hide-and-seek and caught crawdads in the bayou behind our house. There was a sports park with baseball and football fields a ten-minute bike ride away. That's where I had the most fun, playing Little League baseball and Pop Warner football.

Mrs. Ingerman lived next door, a mysterious widow who stayed inside her house alone except when her daughter visited. Then she came outside to water her lawn while her daughter stood by her side. Rumor had it that she had survived the Holocaust and was nervous around people. Mom told me always to be extra nice if I ever needed to speak with her. One afternoon, I accidentally kicked my football over her fence and went to ring her doorbell. She cracked her front door open just enough to peek out but smiled a tiny bit when she saw it was me. She unlocked the side gate to her yard so I could get my football back. I thought she was nice.

The Garner family lived in the house on the other side of us. They went to church every Sunday as we did, except they seemed to like it. They gave away Texas hospitality as good as anyone. Mom was spending more and more time in bed, and they often brought food over when she didn't cook. Whether it was a flat tire or getting the lawnmower to run, they helped with just about anything. I often pictured the Garner family in my mind when I sat in church praying for another family to live with.

The Davidson family lived across the street. They seemed to really like one another and worked together in their yard every weekend. Mrs. Davidson planted flowers while Mr. Davidson mowed and edged the lawn. They had two teenagers: Daniel and Dania. Dania beat the tar out of me in ping-pong. Daniel organized football games on their front lawn with older boys in the neighborhood. He seemed to understand my desire to prove myself. He always picked me for his team, even though I was much younger and smaller than the rest.

"It's your chance to go up against the big dawgs!" he would say.

Every two weeks or so, Mom gave me a dollar to go get a haircut. I'd ride my bike to the barbershop, where I waited my turn and listened to the men talk about cars, sports, politics, and the weather. I enjoyed listening to them and didn't mind the wait. A table in the corner had magazines about cars and boats, hunting and fishing. There was a stack of *LIFE* magazines. What really caught my attention was the day I saw a *Playboy* lying in the pile. I wanted to look at the naked ladies inside but was afraid of what might happen if I got caught. I spent the time waiting by thumbing through the other magazines, pretending I was reading. The owner got a kick out of seeing me pretend to read and let me pick an out-of-date magazine to take home — not the *Playboy, of course!* I folded it lengthwise, stuffed it down the back of my pants, and pedaled home like a madman!

I'd lie on my bed reading and imagine myself catching largemouth bass in the lakes around Texas and deep-sea fishing for marlin off Baja. Or I'd be bagging elk or mule deer in Wyoming's Bitterroot Mountains. I dreamed of what I would do when I was a grown-up. I'd be a big-league catcher in spring and summer. Then a cornerback for either the Dallas Cowboys or the Green Bay Packers in the fall and early winter. In my spare time, I'd be a hunting and fishing guide.

Sunday mornings were a big ordeal every week. We'd all go down the church checklist to make sure we were ready for the show.

Hair washed and combed? *Check!*
Best clothes? *Check!*
Shoes shined? *Check!*
Bible in hand? *Check!*

My father was always nervous on Sundays, and he acted insulted by whoever was the last to get into the car. This was usually my sister. To retaliate, he'd make a snarky remark about what she was wearing. The drive to church ended the same way most every week: my father was red-faced with anger, and my sister was in tears. Once we arrived at church, we put on our smiles as we walked into the building. We were ready to worship and praise the Lord!

As I wrote the early chapters of this book, something deep inside began to push back. I collided with shame head-on and struggled to find the good hidden within the mess of my story. After weeks of frustratingly slow progress, I decided to take a few days off. At 4:30 on a Thursday morning, I threw my leg over my motorcycle, hit the starter button, and headed for the empty backroads of Arizona. Riding motorcycles resets my soul. There's nothing better than barreling down a desert highway on two wheels before sunrise.

As the early morning miles passed, I thought about my family's rules and how they shaped the way I saw myself and the world around me. Two hours later, I pulled up to a restaurant on a side road in the mountains east of San Diego. On the walls inside hung pictures of old Hollywood movie stars. A jukebox played music from the '50s and '60s. I ordered an omelet and drank coffee while I waited. A Beach Boys song began to play, "Good Vibrations." As I hummed the old familiar melody, I thought of how I grew up believing life would be simple and easy as long as I followed *the rules*.

When I was a boy, I knew I'd better get home quick once the streetlights came on. I knew not to leave my bike on the driveway or track mud into the house. I knew to respect adults and never sass my mother or father or tease my sister. I can't say I learned the last one too well. These were straightforward rules I understood without question. If I followed them, I would stay out of trouble. Yet back then, I couldn't begin to know what was going on at a deeper level. I wasn't consciously aware of my family's *unspoken* rules.

If my parents were alive, they would probably tell our family story differently than I'm telling it. My father's version would certainly be dramatically different from my mother's version. I'm not silly enough to think I can tell my sister's story. I am simply telling you what I remember growing up and how it influenced me during those pivotal formative years, and even now somewhat.

Growing old happens to all of us if we're lucky. Just because we grow old doesn't mean we mature. We have to work at it.

So, what were the rules in my home?

Unspoken Rule Number One was that my well-being depended on my father's happiness. He was the all-important one in our family. Everyone in the family honored his importance by keeping him happy.

Unspoken Rule Number Two was that I was a burden to him. He had a not-so-subtle way of letting me know how much he suffered because of the responsibilities he had for our family. He often lectured me when we were driving in his Mustang about how I didn't appreciate the sacrifices he made for me. What was even more clear is that I never understood exactly how I failed him. I was left confused and buried in shame. Even today, his voice still haunts me.

You never appreciate what I've given you.

You never work hard enough.

You're never going to make it!

God forbid I would want more, or ask him for anything.

After breakfast, I saddled up to ride east along the Mexico border. Down from the cool mountain breezes to the warmth of the deserts below. The winds picked up in the flatlands, blowing like a banshee from the north. Sand from the desert dunes blew sideways across the road in sheets like rain, hammering me back and forth on the highway. The faster I rode, the harder I had to work to stay in my lane. If I slowed too much, I risked being blown right over. With little shelter in that part of the desert, I kept going until I crossed the Colorado River into Arizona, where I turned north to ride directly into the wind. Facing the wind head-on made it easier to handle. I relaxed and began to think of my family once again.

My mother played the role of being the sick one in our family. I don't mean to imply that she wanted to be sickly or weak, because I think she was strong — up to a point. Yet over time, the hurtful words my father laid upon her took their toll. She grew blind to her value and lost the will to defend herself. She was an easy scapegoat. With her labeled as *the sick one,* no one noticed the sickness in the rest of us.

My sister made excellent grades and was a joy to be around. She took on the role of our family's happy good student, but my father couldn't tolerate her happiness. He consistently made cutting remarks about her. Even when she was standing beside him in front of other people. "She is thoughtless! She has no respect for my schedule. She needs to wear something suitable."

I can only imagine how such cruelty breaks the tender heart of a young girl.

The earliest message I remember about me was that I was a dullard and a dimwit — a sweet and nice but lazy, never-will-amount-to-anything kind of boy. I grew up believing that I lacked gumption, enterprise, and the smarts to do anything meaningful. So, I worked hard to fit in with others by doing things *for* them. Like changing tires, moving furniture, or setting up chairs at church — sometimes hundreds of them at a time by myself. I was always trying to fit in and always failing to belong.

I SPENT THE FIRST NIGHT of my desert ride in Salome, Arizona. Salome is a tiny dot on the map southwest of Prescott. The next day I was up before sunrise and rode into Prescott for breakfast. There I sat in a coffee shop exploring a route on my GPS that promised lots of curves, with altitude changes and beautiful views of the Arizona outback. It would lead me through rustic lands and deliver me to the iconic town of Seligman.

Once on the road, I'd ridden about seventy miles and hardly seen a car or truck on the road when I came around a bend and saw where the pavement abruptly ended. The road narrowed to a single thin lane of loose dirt and was deeply rutted. It was strewn with rocks and sloped sharply toward deep ditches on both sides. It happened too fast to slow down. I launched off the pavement onto the dirt at over sixty miles an hour. With myself and my gear, my bike weighed more than seven hundred pounds. Every ounce of it violently bucked back and forth.

I immediately began looking for a place to turn around without dumping the bike. If I crashed and was fortunate enough not to be hurt, I'd never be able to pick the bike up without help. The deep ruts and gravel gave me little choice but to keep going down that treacherous road at a slow, steady pace. I rode around bends so tight I couldn't see what might be coming from the opposite direction. I skirted around large boulders that had rolled off the hillsides and fallen trees that lay halfway across the road. A haunting voice whispered to me.

Think how cold it gets out here at night.

No one will look for you; you'll be alone without shelter.

It'll take all night to walk out of here if predators don't get you first.

You'll never make it…

I cursed the terrible road. Then I got mad at myself for cursing and started cussing at myself. In anger and frustration, I looked down at my GPS to find where I was. I had traveled about twenty miles. Then I realized I was still upright and okay. *Look how far I've come!*

I pressed on with my slow and steady pace. A little while later, I glanced again at my GPS. It showed forty-three more miles to Seligman. *If I don't stop…if I don't rush too fast and crash, I will get there.*

I took a deep breath and accepted the slow pace the road would allow. Rounding a turn, I saw a coyote in hot pursuit chasing a rabbit across the road right in front of me. Startled, I flinched in the saddle but then snickered: *Good for him. Old Wile E. has finally given up on roadrunners!*

Two and a half hours later, I crested a rise and saw semitrucks in the far distance, heading east toward Flagstaff. My tires soon left the gravel of that rutted dirt road, landing on perfect asphalt just south of Seligman. Soaked with sweat,

I didn't stop for a second. I craved a shower, a meal, and a safe place for the night.

I thought about that rock-strewn road and its deep ruts for weeks. In hindsight, I could have stopped and turned around on several occasions, but I kept going anyway. I felt scared when faced with the unexpected, but I wanted adventure and needed to prove something to myself along the way.

Autumn Shame

FROM THE TIME I WAS A YOUNG BOY, I've always loved the first chill of autumn. It signaled the end of summer's heat, and the Houston rains felt cool when they poured down. I was walking home from second grade on such an afternoon. The air was crisp, and the rain was heavy. The wind howled like a demon. I felt the electricity in the air as lightning crashed close over my head. As I turned the corner onto Sandpiper Street, I looked ahead and saw it was flooded in front of our house. I walked the rest of the way in water up to my waist.

Under the weight of my father's abuse, Mom was sinking ever deeper into despair, and she was in bed asleep when I got home. Her bottle of Valium was on her nightstand. Always quick with boyhood make-believe, I saw this as my chance to escape and *go fishing.* I grabbed my Zebco and went back outside.

The tree in our front yard heaved back and forth in the wind. It was the tallest in the neighborhood, taller than the highest point of our roof. The leaves had fallen, and the branches rode the winds up and down like a surfer rides the waves. The smaller branches at the top were gnarled and bent, clawing at the gray sky.

I found a large washer in our garage closet — where my father kept his gardening tools. I took the washer and tied it to the nylon string of my Zebco. I left the garage and walked to the curb in water above my knees. Reaching back, I cast the line and washer into the waters flowing down the street. I imagined the flowing waters were a lake, and I was casting a baited hook to entice a largemouth bass. Once that bass struck, I imagined reeling it in and cooking it over a campfire like the fishermen in the barbershop magazines.

That stormy afternoon fishing in the street was fantastic. I couldn't get enough of the chilly, wet joy of casting my line into the flooded street over and over again. With each cast, the line of my Zebco made an enticing sound.

Whiz-zing kerplunk! Whiz-zing kerplunk!

I loved how that sound mixed right along with the wind and thunder.

Our church had recently been publicizing a Saturday fellowship at one of the lakes north of the city. It was a picnic outing with boating and fishing. Fishing was all I needed to hear; I was all in! One thousand and ten percent! As far as I was concerned, it made perfect sense to stand in the cold rain to practice my casting even with crashing lightning and booming thunder close by.

Between casts, I noticed Mrs. Davidson across the street, standing in her doorway, looking at me. Then I saw Mr. Davidson, in his fishing waders, wearing a rain slicker and cap, wading across the flooded street toward me. As he came closer, I could hear the rain on his head and shoulders. *Poppity-poppity-pop!*

"Whatcha doin', David?" he asked.

"I'm gettin' ready," I said and cast the line again. *Whiz-zing kerplunk!*

"I'm going fishing," I explained. "We're going to the lake with my church. I'm going to catch a bass, and my mom will cook it for supper!"

"Son, I don't think you're gonna catch anything out here but a bad cold — if you don't get struck by lightning first."

"Well, yes, sir. I know, but I'm just doing it for practice."

I reeled in the line to show him the washer on the end of it — feeling ridiculous but trying not to look it.

"With this lightning and all, you better get back inside."

Mr. Davidson made his point clear by nudging me gently toward the front door of our house.

A couple of days later, Daniel and I were tossing a football back and forth on their front lawn after school when Mr. Davidson called us into his garage. He lifted a metal box off his workbench. It looked like an old rusty lunch pail. He handed it to me and said, "Open it."

I set the box on the garage floor but struggled to get the latch to open. Once it finally released, I raised the lid to look inside. There were two fishing bobbers, one foam and one plastic, plus a few lead weights and fishing hooks like the ones Mr. Hargis used.

"I sorted through my tackle box this morning," Mr. Davidson said, "and thought you could use this for your fishing trip. You want it?"

Of course, you know I wanted that box. I felt like I had just opened a treasure chest, but my mouth couldn't get out a simple "Yes, sir!" Instead, I stared at the garage floor feeling embarrassed, and wondered, *Is this a Candid Camera episode? Was Allen Funt about to jump out and say, "Surprise!" while the whole world watched my stupid humiliation on TV?*

It was all I could do not to grab that rusty tackle box and run away like a thief with his loot.

Seeing my hesitation, Mr. Davidson bent down, picked the tackle box up off the floor, and set it on his workbench. As Daniel and I watched, he took one of his fishing poles and showed us how to slip the bobbers on the line and attach the weights in proper length to the bobber.

Then he said, "Watch this close now!" and he tied a hook on the line using a clinch knot.

"See that?" he asked. "I'll show you again."

He snipped the hook off the line and retied it once more. I watched him as carefully as I knew how. He then handed the hook and line to me. "Here. Do it for yourself."

It took a few tries, with my fingers getting tangled in the line while he and Daniel watched. With a bit of coaching, I tied my first clinch knot and felt confident I was ready to catch me a bass at the lake.

I had no idea of the coming storm.

THE DAY BEFORE we were supposed to go to the lake, my father came home and said, "Things have come up. I can't go tomorrow." He went on to say that Mom wasn't up to driving there and back by herself. This now is not surprising to me in the least. My father liked fishing as much as he wanted a hole drilled into his head. When he saw the look of disappointment on my face, he called his friend from the church choir, Gene Lang, and arranged for Gene to pick me up and take me along with him. "There," said my father as he put down the phone. "I took care of it. Now you can do all the fishing you want."

He then drove me to a store that sold bait, where he bought me a box of worms.

"Don't you open that in this car," he said as we got into his Mustang to go home.

We arrived back home right at suppertime, but I ignored my mother's call to the table. I ran to the garage, where I opened the box of worms and reached into the mucky ooze. Those wonderful squiggly worms wrapped themselves all around my fingers.

Wormy camouflage! Perfect for hiding hooks from fish like Mr. Hargis showed me!

I put the worms in my tackle box and set it outside our front door along with my Zebco, so I could grab 'em quick when Gene Lang arrived the next morning.

I hardly slept a wink that night. Once I finally drifted off, I heard *whiz-zing kerplunk* in my dreams and saw myself reeling in one fish after another. *Saturday will be another best day ever.* I was sure it was going to be just like when I went fishing with Mr. Hargis.

The following morning, I was up and out of bed before anyone. It was a cool autumn day, without a cloud in the sky as the sun came up. Halfway through my third bowl of Cap'n Crunch cereal, Mom walked into the kitchen. She saw the cereal and immediately put it away and started cooking eggs and bacon, which I forced down even though I was already stuffed to the gills with cereal. My father left to do whatever he needed to do, and I waited for Gene to arrive. I waited and waited and waited.

Gene finally showed up mid-morning. I immediately recognized his face when I looked out the window and saw him coming to our door. His seat in the choir was behind my father at the organ, and he attended every church social. He was quick with a hug and a joke as he guzzled punch and ate sugar cookies by the handful.

He greeted my mom with a hug. Then he carried on about how bad the traffic was for a Saturday morning before putting my Zebco and tackle box into the trunk of his car, next to folding chairs and a cooler. Mom gave me a hug and a kiss, then she handed me the new winter coat she'd recently bought for me and said, "Put it on!"

She stood at our door smiling and waving as we backed out the driveway. I waved back.

The lake was about forty miles north of Houston. Gene talked nonstop all the way. I sat in silence. Once he realized I wasn't a talker, he turned on the car radio and tuned the knob to a gospel station. I had never ridden in a car so nice, with cushy white seats and pleated padding on the doors to match. I couldn't help but notice the floorboards. They were covered in plush blue carpet. The music from the radio came through as loud and clear as a concert hall. Gene suddenly broke out singing gospel praise at the top of his lungs, making me jump in my seat. It was a joyful noise at best and reminded me of the way Vesta hummed her hymns, only a whole lot louder. I wanted to cover my ears, but I was afraid it would hurt his feelings.

There were a few dozen people already at the lake when we arrived. Hot dogs and hamburgers were sizzling on the grills. Bowls of potato salad and beans sat on the picnic tables alongside paper plates and napkins. A lady stood next to the table waving paper plates in the air to keep the flies away. Gene took the chairs and cooler out of his trunk. He left my Zebco and tackle box as he began hugging people and telling jokes while he set up his chairs.

I saw a boat dock at the edge of the lake and ran straight for it. It was about fifty feet long. Tied to it were two small aluminum boats with outboard motors. I walked to the very end and lay down to reach my hand into the water. The lumber of the dock felt warm beneath me from the sun, but the water felt cold to my hand. I was lying there looking into the water for fish when I heard Gene call me. People were sitting down to eat, so I went back and sat next to him on one of his folding chairs. A lady I recognized from church said, "Hey, you're Lew Zailer's boy!" as she handed me a hot dog and a napkin, and a bottle of Coca-Cola.

After what seemed like hours, Gene finally said, "Well, folks, time for us to get moving. David here wants to go fishing. I best get him out there and see what he can catch."

I was out of that chair in a flash!

Gene went to his car to get my Zebco and tackle box from the trunk, then we walked down to the dock and hopped into one of the boats. No one mentioned a thing about life vests. It was 1966, a much freer, risk-taking world. With a few mighty yanks of the cord, the motor sputtered to life. It belched blue-gray smoke into the air as we set out.

I sat at the front of the boat, and Gene steered at the rear. There were many other boats on the lake. I wondered if we should go where they had gathered, but Gene seemed sure of where he was going. I sat there with my hand over the side, feeling the cold water as we glided through it. The wind was cold on my face. Mom was right; I was glad I had my winter coat.

We rounded a bend in the lake and motored into a small cove. Gene slowed the throttle and steered the boat to the side, putting its nose up on the bank. "Hop on out. I want to show you something," he said.

I scrambled out and grabbed the rope connected to the front of the boat. Gene stepped out. I handed him the rope, he tied it to a tree just off the bank. Once the boat was secured, Gene began walking through a thicket of tall grass much higher than my head. Not knowing where he was going, I followed him, using my arms in sweeping motions to push the grass aside. We had made our way fifty or so yards into the thicket when Gene abruptly turned around. His pants were unzipped. His penis was out. He reached behind my neck, pulled me toward him, and put it into my mouth.

For many years, I called myself stupid for going into that thicket behind him that day. Even now, my mind sometimes goes blank when I remember it. Then I see the image of a bloody and unconscious child buried alive in the rubble of what used to be his home after an evil act of war crushed it.

GENE AND I MOTORED BACK across the lake to the picnic grounds late in the day as the sun began to go down. The temperature was falling. The wind was like an icy knife. Looking ahead, I saw the church folk still gathered at the picnic area. I counted the seconds until I could get out of the boat.

As we came near, I jumped for the dock with my Zebco in one hand and my tackle box in the other. I leapt too early and fell far short, tumbling into the frigid water. I was a good swimmer for eight, but the cold instantly took my breath away. Weighed down by my coat, I began to sink. I instinctively let go of my Zebco and tackle box and began clawing my way back up to the surface. Just as my head broke above the water, a man grabbed one of my flailing arms. He took hold of my collar and hauled me up on the dock. I was chilled to the bone but safe, considering everything else. My beloved Zebco and tackle box had sunk to the bottom. They were gone.

I sat in the back seat of Gene's car on the way home, wrapped in a blanket someone had put around me, my teeth chattering. Gene had stowed my coat in the trunk because it was too wet for the inside of his car. He stopped on the way and used a pay phone outside a gas station.

"I called your father to let him know you jumped out of the boat, but everything's OK."

My parents greeted us at the door. I stood there holding my soaked coat in hand as my father apologized to Gene for the trouble I had caused. He promised that I would learn a lesson from my mistake and never be a bother again. Mom put me into the tub and then straight to bed. Tomorrow was Sunday. *The show had to go on.*

I didn't tell a soul about that day for thirty years. All the while, I wondered if I was a coward, especially as I grew older and saw others come forward to tell similar stories. Back in the 1960s, no one talked of such things. There was no discussion or conversation to help us understand what had happened. There was always the hidden question.

Who could understand?

And after seeing what happened when my mother asked my father and Vesta for help, I was afraid of being called crazy like my father said she was. My father never believed my mother. Why would he believe me?

Silence is a well-worn survival skill, but it doesn't work for long.

The following year, when I was nine and in the third grade, some of the men from church planned to take their sons to an Astros game at the Astrodome. As an ambitious Little Leaguer, I wanted to go so bad, but my father had less interest in baseball than fishing. Can you guess who offered to take me? I thought it impossible for lightning to strike twice, but I was wrong.

And again, when I was ten and in the fourth grade, I was often set out in the hallway outside by the Sunday School teachers as punishment because my behavior was unbearable. My classmates watched with befuddled stares as the teacher set my chair in the hallway, pointed to it for me to sit, and closed the classroom door behind them. Gene saw me sitting there alone one week and took me to a sports court area of the church that was *off-limits* on Sunday mornings.

There's no need to tell you more.

Everything changed for me after that day at the lake. When I looked outside and saw Daniel and the older boys playing football, I wanted to go out and join them, but instead, I stayed inside watching TV. Rather than riding bikes with my buddies, I spent hours peddling to new areas beyond the neighborhood by myself. Bicycle maintenance had usually been a social event for all the boys living on Sandpiper Street. We would meet on a friend's driveway and work side by side, patching inner tubes, changing tires, and adjusting and oiling the chains on our bikes. After the lake, I preferred to fix my bike alone, using whatever tools I could find in our garage at home.

About two weeks after the lake, I was looking in my father's garage closet for a wrench to work on my bike: the same closet where I had found the washer for practicing casts. I didn't find what I needed. Instead, I found pornography wrapped in a brown paper bag stashed away, hidden on a shelf. The magazines were filled with glossy full-color pages of beautiful women and handsome men in explicit sex acts and similar magazines of young men having sex with other young men. The mind-numbing images were more than I could make sense of as a young boy. I wondered who would keep such images hidden secretly away in the garage closet of my home.

Yet then again, beyond my innocence and denial, I knew the porn belonged to my father. Who else could it be?

After finding my father's porn, I remember sitting in church feeling frightened as I listened to the preacher's sermon. I knew it was hopeless; I was going to hell. I would look around at the men and wonder:

Were they like Gene?

Were they like my father?

I'm not sure what hurt me more: Gene's sexual assaults against me or learning my father used porn to cheat on my mother.

From time to time during those childhood years, I'd sneak into the garage closet to see if his porn was still there. Some of the magazines would be gone but replaced by new ones. Their cost was astonishing. Each of them had a price tag of twenty-five dollars or more. A small fortune for a modest family in the 1960s, especially given how my father complained to us, "You all spend my hard-earned money like it was water!"

I kept his pornography secret until I was thirteen, when I told my sister. We both kept it secret for another year until she finally exposed him. It started as one of their screaming matches. To counter my father's aggression, she ran to the garage and pulled out his porn. She came back into the house and threw it in his face! Mom and I watched it happen, but she wasn't surprised. She simply grabbed her Valium bottle from the kitchen cupboard and went down the hall to bed. I shot out the front door and didn't come back until the morning.

The next day, my father sat me down to explain. "Your mother is cold and unloving. I need something to help me. I'm sure you'll understand someday."

My father's pornography use didn't end there. I lived in my parents' home until I was eighteen and found porn stashed around the house in the oddest places. He had secret hiding places all over. The way some alcoholics hide their booze.

I think of the nature of childhood curiosity and the need to make sense of things we don't comprehend. I'd look at the women in my father's pornography with longing and desire for their beauty, and I envied the men for being naked with them. When seeing men having sex with other men — although I'm not sure the "men" in my father's porn were adults, because they looked very young — I was trying to make sense of what Gene had done to me.

It was all very confusing to me.

SIMON WAS MY BEST FRIEND at Sutton Elementary. His family was Jewish and went to their synagogue as often as my family went to our church. We were terrors on the kickball field and often sat together at the lunch table to gloat about our success. I noticed that Simon's lunch box was packed full each day. He would have sandwiches layered thick with meat and cheese and lettuce and tomato, along with an apple or orange, and a pudding cup with a plastic spoon and napkin. I watched how his mother met him at the curb after school with a hug. All this made me envy Simon, so I decided I wanted to be Jewish like him. I went so far as telling my classmates and teachers that I was. I didn't stop there. One Sunday, an old lady at church asked me, "What are you going to be when you grow up, David?"

"I'm going to be Jewish and play for the Dallas Cowboys!" I replied.

I bet you know how that went over. Mom was standing right next to me, and she was beyond embarrassed. She corrected me, "Now, don't be a fibber, David!"

My childhood fibs didn't stop with being Jewish or having grandiose dreams of being a football star. I told the story of how my mother had been an international beauty queen in

117

her hometown of Cheyenne, Wyoming, and runner-up in the Miss America pageant. I told anyone who would listen that my father had been an internationally famous pianist who fell head over heels in love with my mother. Because of his great love for her, he quit his career to marry her and start a family. Perhaps most outlandish of all, I told my schoolmates about hunting grizzly bears with my father on the weekends, and how we had skinned one to make a rug for our family room. Of course, no one believed the tall tales I told. Other boys challenged my lies, which led to the dustups at Cub Scouts. One reason for my expulsion, you remember. More severe fisticuffs happened after school and resulted in black eyes and bloody lips. I quickly learned to always dish it out stronger and faster to the other guy than he did to me.

I even told a colossal whopper to Mr. Davidson. I had been avoiding him because I didn't want him to know that I'd lost the tackle box he had given me. One day, he was watering his lawn as I came home on my bike, so I couldn't avoid him. I told him about a terrible storm that blew across the lake the day we were fishing, how the boat sank, and how I had to swim for my life. "Whew! Lucky for me, I'm a strong swimmer and survived. Most horrible of all, the tackle box you gave me and my Zebco went down with the boat, along with the three bass and two catfish I'd caught."

Because of my lying and fighting, I was often sent to the principal's office or the school counselor's office for meetings with my parents. Mom cried, and my father seethed. The school demanded corrective measures and referred my parents to professionals. Soon I was seeing doctors several times a week. I was poked and prodded and once even sedated so they could shave my hair in spots where wires were then glued to my head.

"We have to take a nice picture of your brain," the nurse explained to me.

I also had several appointments with a psychiatrist to "just talk."

Once the assessments were completed, my diagnosis came: *Mentally Retarded.*

Medication was prescribed to control my behavior, but it only grew worse.

Ultimately, I was reassigned to a special school for troubled children.

My name became *Retard.*

I RETURNED TO HOUSTON for more work on a cloudy Sunday afternoon in the fall. On my way from the airport to the hotel, I stopped at Walmart to buy an umbrella because rain was on the way. When I checked in at the front desk, I noticed a flower arrangement set on a pedestal in the middle of the lobby. It was extraordinary, so I walked over for a closer look. When I saw it up close, I thought of the roses I had first taken to my mother's grave, which now seemed cheap by comparison. Comparison often reminds me how the shame of inadequacy lurks close by wherever I am.

A small silver tray next to the flowers held business cards for the shop that sold them. I slipped one into my pocket, deciding right then and there to buy flowers from this shop and visit Mom at the cemetery before work in the morning.

I jogged at sunrise in light rain, plodding my way through wet autumn leaves that covered the sidewalk. After showering, I ate breakfast at the hotel, punched the flower shop address into the GPS, and set off. Finding the flower shop in a strip mall, I dashed in the rain from the car to the storefront. When I pushed the door open, a bell sounded. *Ding-dong!*

I stepped inside, breathing in the earthy aroma of plants and flowers. On the left side of the store, small trees grew in whiskey barrels cut in half. On the other side were rows of miniature bonsai plants in small handmade pots. I picked one up to examine it and almost keeled over at the price. I sure wasn't looking to spend that kind of money. I was just hoping to buy a quick bouquet and get to the cemetery.

I saw glass doors to a lighted room filled with flowers of every color at the rear of the store. Then I heard tiny footsteps from the back coming toward me, timed in unison with a rhythmic jingle that sounded like a pocketful of change. *Ching-ching-ching-ching.* A small woman with a big smile appeared. She wasn't close to a hundred pounds, even soaking wet. She had thick gray hair pulled back into a ponytail that hung to her waist. Her face was lean and creased with well-formed lines of experience, and a red dot was centered between her eyebrows. She wore a multicolored dress made of silk and several bracelets on each wrist — which accounted for the *ching-ching* sounds — and a small gold stud in the side of her nose. Gold earrings dangled from each ear. Her brown eyes shined clear and bright like sunlight shining through colored glass.

"Hello, hello. Welcome to my store," the woman said with a thick Indian accent.

"Good morning, I need some flowers," I replied. "I want something nice."

She took a small step back and put a hand over her mouth. "Oh my, I'm so sorry, but we don't have any flowers to sell yet this morning. Can I interest you in a lovely tree?"

Apparently I was missing something, I thought.

The woman immediately recognized my confusion and said, "I'm sorry, let me explain. We only sell fresh flowers, and they only come in every three days. The flowers you see in the back are three days old already and will be thrown out when the new ones arrive. Could you come back in an hour? Or how about a nice miniature plant? They look great in the office!"

"Ma'am, everything looks quite nice, but I only need flowers for the grave of a loved one," I said. "And I'm on a schedule this morning. I'll be more than happy with the flowers you have now."

She took another step back and dropped her jaw open wide enough that I could see the gold on her back teeth.

"Oh, I'm so sorry, and I feel so bad for you," she said. "I don't like selling flowers that aren't fresh, but I understand your sadness and will make an exception just for you."

"Thank you," I replied. "But they've been dead for thirty years. I'd just like to take some flowers now while I have the time this morning."

She nodded and started toward the glass room in the back. I followed her, but in a few steps, she stopped abruptly, turned back toward me, and took hold of my arm. Leaning up on her toes, she whispered into my ear as if to tell me a secret. "The time someone is in the ground doesn't matter much, does it?" she asked. "It's how they live on with us and how we live on with ourselves that makes the difference. I'm sure you know this already of course. Isn't this why you need the flowers?"

She then did something odd. She took my hand as if I were a child and led me to view the flowers behind the glass doors. She held out her other hand toward them as if in a grand gesture and declared, "Choose whatever pleases you. I'll make you two for the price of one."

My eyes were drawn to a bushel of bright yellow flowers, and I pointed at them.

"I like those," I announced. "They're sunny and cheerful. Thank you for your generosity, but I don't need two for one. One is all I want, thank you."

"Excellent!" she said with a grin, slapping her hands together playfully. *Ching-ching.*

When she slid the glass doors open, the cool air flowed out. She thoughtfully selected a number of the yellow flowers and flowers of other colors as well. She slid the glass doors closed and disappeared through a doorway curtained by strings of hanging beads. As she arranged the flowers in the back, the sound of her bracelets chimed in the air. *Ching-ching. Ching-ching.*

I moseyed about the store while I waited. The cash register was behind a counter. On the wall behind the counter were small pictures of the American flag, Texas's flag, and India's flag. I hadn't noticed him before, but right below the flags sat a frail, white-haired man. He was silent and motionless except for a pencil he moved across a piece of paper that intently held his interest. I felt stupid for not seeing him sooner but thought this would be a good moment to clear up any confusion. "Good morning, sir. I see that you are busy, and I'm terribly sorry to bother you, but I don't really need two sets of flowers. I'd prefer just one. Since they're not fresh, could I possibly, maybe, have a discount instead?"

The man didn't even look up. He slowly pulled his glasses from his face and let them fall against his chest, held by a string around his neck. He then dropped his pencil onto the desk in a way that let me know I was a nuisance to him. He stood slowly from his chair with a groan and held the back of it to steady his balance. With wobbly steps, he made his way through the beaded doorway, mumbling as he shuffled to where his wife was busy at work.

The *ching-ching* stopped, and I heard them speaking in their Indian language. Moments later, the old man reappeared, mumbling even more. He wobbled his way back to the register and stood doddering as he continued to mutter. As I watched him, I realized: *He's cussing me under his breath!*

He began pushing the keys on the register, studying each button with great care. I watched as he struggled and I thought about his life. He didn't appear to be terribly old. I wondered what had made him so rickety and disagreeable. Then I remembered how cranky I could be and felt a measure of compassion for him.

When he finished the register entry, the total came up on the screen.

"That'll be seventy-one dollars and seventy-five cents total with tax!" He glared.

How much? I thought. But I didn't want an argument, so I paid quickly while forcing a smile back in his direction.

The lady reappeared a few minutes later with two flower bouquets. They were more beautiful than I could have imagined. She held one in each of her hands as she walked toward me. She thrust the bouquets into my hands with such force I had to step back to steady myself. She then grabbed the sleeve of my jacket and pulled me toward the entrance. At the front door, she grabbed it with both hands and pulled it open with all her might. The rain had grown heavy. It was now loud and pouring down.

Holding the door for me, she beamed. "Look at that rain come down! Isn't it a great day for you to be happy?"

I ZIPPED THE BOUQUETS inside my jacket and sprinted for the car in the soaking rain. I set them on the back seat, started the car, clicked the wipers on high, and headed for the cemetery. I thought about the old man as I drove. Thinking of him made me think of my father. It was just past nine in the morning, and I already felt exhausted. The ongoing weight of my life, and the way I had remembered it, was an emotional burden I couldn't carry anymore.

I asked myself, "Why do I keep heaping this horror upon myself? Do I want to stay stuck, or do I want to move on?"

Enough! I heard myself say. *I'm tired of remembering things the way I have. The pain of my past experiences will never change until I change the way I see it.*

I parked at the cemetery in the usual spot and listened to the rain as it pounded the roof of the car. The deluge sounded like marbles crashing down from the sky. It layered thick on the windshield and ran down in streaks, blurring the image of everything outside.

Listening to the rain made me think of my father and the tree in our front yard on Sandpiper Street that he loved so much.

When I was ten, I was selected by our local Little League coaches to advance and play on a team with boys two and three years older than me. I was thrilled with the challenge, especially since I had been labeled mentally retarded the year before. Of course, that was a secret I kept from my teammates. I worked hard to deserve my spot on the team, riding my bike to practice early and staying late to run extra bases. I was always trying to impress the coaches. On Sunday afternoons, my teammates and their fathers went to the batting cages for extra batting practice. I wanted to join them badly but never did. Since batting practice interfered with Sunday night church, my father wouldn't allow it. I never argued or complained because of the guilt I felt for daring to violate church values. I kept the disappointment to myself, harboring it deep in my ten-year-old heart.

One day after summer school, I found a can of white paint and a brush in the garage closet. Yes, the same closet where my father stashed his porn. Measuring my beltline to the tree, I took the paint and brushed a dot the size of a baseball on the tree trunk. I took my batting stance and imagined a fastball coming down the middle of the plate. I swung my bat as hard as I could, as if hitting a home run, striking the tree. *Thunk!* The bat vibrated painfully in my hands, but I didn't stop. I kept swinging at imaginary fastballs, hitting imaginary home runs, repeatedly striking the tree. *Thunk! Thunk! Thunk!* I kept hitting the tree until I suddenly realized: *I've beaten a hole into the tree the size of home plate.*

I know today that whacking the side of the tree was not totally about baseball. It was about retaliation. *Rage and revenge!*

My father loved that tree, and I knew it. He often remarked how "his tree" made our house look good, and it shaded the room where he kept his piano and organ, which kept him cool and comfortable while he practiced.

So I pounded the crap out of his tree.

Thunder clapped outside. I looked through the rain on the windows and saw the wind in the trees, then checked my watch. I needed to get to work soon. *I'll take the extra bouquet to the office — bright, sunny flowers on a stormy day. The ladies will love me!*

I opened the car door, then my umbrella, and stepped out. As I pulled the rear door open and saw the two bouquets on the seat, a familiar voice inside asked, *"What are you going to do now? What will you do with your pain?"*

I paused to think for a moment, but before I could change my mind, I grabbed both bouquets. I held them tight against my chest as I walked through the rain-soaked grass until I arrived at my parents' headstone. I set one bouquet beside my mother's name. That was an easy joy and I smiled when I did it. Rain poured down heavier than ever as I stood there.

I clutched the last bouquet tighter against my chest as I turned to my father's name on the headstone. Long unspoken words emerged inside me. *As long as I hold you in contempt, I hold myself in contempt. What would it be like if I were to dig deep and find something worthy in you? Perhaps I'll find something worthy in me.*

After a moment's hesitation, I gritted my teeth and wondered what the future might hold.

I let go of anger for the moment and set the flowers down next to my father's name.

WINTER GRIEF

WHEN I ARRIVED BACK HOME after the second trip to Houston, I pulled another photo from the manila envelope and pinned it to the wall in my office. It was a photocopy of a family portrait of my mother and her family from the early 1940s. I placed it to the left of the picture of Andrew and me. It hung opposite the photo of my father and his family that I pinned up after my first trip to Houston.

In the photo, my mother was about nine or ten years old. Even as a child in the picture, her face reflected sadness. I thought of the sadness I felt at the same age. I studied the faces of my mother's family in the picture like I did with my father and his family in their photo, but I felt entirely different about what I remembered. I only remembered that one trip to visit Vesta, but I remembered many visits to my mother's childhood home.

My mother was born Betty Pauline Haines in 1932 to Paul and Ruth Haines. My grandparents were Kansas farm kids who married young with ambitions of love and family. I knew them simply as Grandma and Grandpa. Mom was their fourth of five children. She grew up to be a quiet young woman with family ambitions of her own. Everyone knew her as Polly.

The first time I remember visiting Grandma and Grandpa's house was before the age of five, and the last was at the age of twelve. They lived on Warren Avenue in Cheyenne, Wyoming. Cheyenne was a quintessential American town on the eastern prairie, just north of the Colorado line. Pronghorn antelope roamed the grassland prairies outside of town, along with range cattle and feral horses. As a boy, one of my lifelong ambitions was to be a cowboy. Cheyenne was my gateway to the Wild West.

Every July, Cheyenne hosts the world-famous Frontier Days Rodeo, where I watched awestruck as cowboys battled bucking broncs and raging bulls. Whenever we drove into town for a visit, I looked out the backseat window of my father's Mustang and imagined myself patrolling those prairies on horseback. With my .45 revolver holstered against my thigh and my Winchester 44 rifle sheathed beside my saddle, I would be ever vigilant for cattle rustlers and marauding bandits.

The dairyman delivered milk and eggs each morning before sunrise. He stowed them in a box at the front door to keep them from freezing in winter. A few blocks away was a hardware store, a barbershop, a beauty salon, a grocery store, and a pet store. After the fishing trip with Gene, my mother and I spent a good portion of the summer in Cheyenne. I realize now it was a separation of sorts between my parents. I'm sure they would never have called it that because of their religious convictions, but we were there for weeks while my father remained in Houston. I didn't understand it then, but now I see why my mother wanted extended time away from my father.

Mom and I often walked to the center of town for groceries and other necessities to help Grandma with the household chores. On one walk, I noticed in the pet store window a small white dog alone and hiding behind its water dish. I begged and pleaded with my mom to buy me the little dog. She understood how sad I was when my father gave Blacky away, so she gave in to my pleas and bought the puppy for me. I named my new dog Whitey Ford after the pitcher from the New York Yankees, but I just called him Whitey. Whitey and I spent hours playing together in the side yard of my grandparent's home. When Mom and I took the long bus ride back to Houston at the end of that summer's visit, Whitey sat devotedly alongside me.

Arriving back in Houston, I was already counting the days until the next trip back to Cheyenne to be with my grandparents.

When we'd pull up to their house on the next visit, I'd jump out of the car and run to my grandfather as fast as I could. He'd pick me up and throw me over his shoulder with a long, exaggerated groan. "O Lord, help me! You're getting too big, David!"

My grandfather's love for me always made Mom smile.

In the winter, Grandpa shoveled snow from the walkway and the sidewalks with the efficiency of a finely tuned machine. He'd often shovel the neighbor's sidewalk too.

"I need to work off your grandma's cooking," he'd cheer-fully say.

Grandpa preferred denim pants and inexpensive short-sleeve shirts. I'd hang out with him in the garage while he worked on his car. He would tell elaborate stories about delivering calves and driving a tractor on the farm where he grew up. On his days off in the summer, he would mow the lawn and touch up the paint on their house and the white picket fence that separated their yard from the alley that ran beside the house. He always took great care not to damage the rosebushes that Grandma grew next to the fence. Her roses were her spring and summer joy.

Mom often put on old work clothes to work alongside Grandpa. One day they were painting the fence along the alley while I was playing in the yard with Whitey. Grandpa suddenly tumbled face-first into the grass. The bucket of paint he was carrying splashed everywhere. Mom heard the commotion and turned to look. When she saw him lying there, she screamed, "Pop! Pop!"

Tears began to flow down her face as she ran toward him. His body was limp, and he looked dead as a doornail as she strained to roll him onto his back. I stood there, frozen in place. As Mom sobbed, a slight smile formed on the sides of my grandpa's mouth that quickly grew into a chuckle and then into full, boisterous laughter, like one of the happy clowns at the circus.

Relieved, my mother started hitting my grandpa on his shoulders and chest but soon stopped to wipe the tears from her face. They both sat and leaned against the fence, covered in paint, laughing hysterically together. It was so clear for me to see that Grandpa enjoyed having Mom around.

Towering oak trees canopied the front yard of my grandparent's home. The trees were full of squirrels, which Grandpa trained to eat from his hand. I sat beside him on the front steps, as still as I could be, while he held a peanut in his scarred and dirty hand, patiently waiting for the next squirrel to take it. The squirrels were quicker than quick to notice the peanut prize. As I watched spellbound, they made their herky-jerky way down from the tops of the trees and up the walkway to snatch the nutty prize from his bear-paw hand. Then, they turned and dashed back to the treetops, chattering and swishing their bushy tails in triumphant victory.

My grandma hated "those dirty varmints." She ranted loud and long about their filth and disease. When we came back inside, she immediately made us wash our hands and arms up to our elbows with soap and hot water. Grandpa never argued, but he kept feeding the squirrels anyway.

Grandpa was diagnosed with cancer in his sixties. It took him fast, just one year after Mom bought me Whitey Ford. On the day he died, I sat in the hospital waiting room as Mom said goodbye to him. When she left his room, I remember her walking down the hallway toward me in tears. If there was any hurt between my mother and my grandpa, I believe they worked it out before he died.

Back in my office, I looked at my grandpa's face in the picture again. For the first time, I saw how much I look like him. I have his jawline. I was built strong and lean like him as a younger man. His eyes were dark brown like my mother's, and mine are blue, but now that I'm in my early sixties, I see how our eyelids sag in much the same way. I like to think that I have his eyes. I also noticed a familiar gentleness on his face. I remember him punishing me several times for rough-housing indoors and how he wouldn't tolerate a hint of any sass to my mother or grandma. Even when he disciplined me, I felt the gentle restraint in him.

I knew he loved me. This made all the difference.

Looking at the pictures on the wall of my father and grandpa, I thought of the profound difference in the way they both used their hands.

My father had two great fears: hurting his hands and tarnishing his image. My grandpa's hands were calloused like leather. His greatest fear was that he might fail his family. I don't think he wasted two seconds thinking about his image.

I find myself stuck in the middle between these two men.

I can't avoid the questions that arise in my heart.

What kind of man am I?

What do I fear the most?

LIFE BACK AT HOME on Sandpiper Street was never quiet and simple the way I remember it with my grandparents in Cheyenne. Angry sounds continued to come through the wall at night from my parents' bedroom. It was never worse than the night before I started the fourth grade. The following morning, the anger didn't stop when I heard the front door slam and the engine of my father's Mustang roar as he sped off to work.

For weeks, I had known that I would be going to a new school. The reality didn't hit home until Mom left me at the kitchen table eating cereal while she walked my sister two blocks to Sutton Elementary. When she returned, we got into her car to drive to the school the doctors and school administrators recommended. We passed Sutton Elementary as we left our neighborhood, and panic broadsided me. I began to shout, "What's wrong with you? Dad's right! You're stupid! You're crazy for doing this to me!"

It was a thirty-minute drive, and I didn't stop screaming at her until we pulled into the parking lot. Though I resisted as best I could, she dragged me to the school office, where she met with a school administrator behind closed doors while I sat on a wooden bench outside his office. As my feet dangled beneath me, I kept thinking of the time my mother and father were arguing in our living room. I remember my father turning and shaking the rolled-up newspaper in my face. "He doesn't need any help. He needs a good spanking he'll never forget!"

When my mother and the administrator walked out of the office, the administrator said to me, "So, David, I heard you've had a difficult morning. I trust all that is behind us now. Are you ready?"

I shrugged while kicking one foot back and forth across the floor.

The administrator led me out a back door of the building and down a gravel path. The classroom was at the back of the school grounds, about seventy-five yards away. The gravel made gritty sounds beneath our feet as we walked. *Crunch, crunch, crunch.* In my mind, I can still see that the grass along the path was wet from overnight rains. Huge mud puddles were everywhere. We came to a converted mobile home set up on blocks, with the wheels removed. The windows were painted over black. No one could see inside or out.

A sign hung on the door. *Private — Special Education.*

Someone should have added: *Penitentiary.*

The class combined grades three through six. Our desks sat in a circle but were partitioned from one another and faced the teacher's desk in the center of the room. Light bulbs hung from the ceiling with strings hanging down to switch them on or off. My new classmates, eight to ten in number and both boys and girls, were as different from one another as could be. I remember three of them well.

There was Stanley, a sixth-grader, who sat quietly for hours on end but then would erupt in the blink of an eye with arms flailing and legs kicking while spewing profanity and barking like a dog. The teacher was quick to scold him, and she would do it without mercy. I jumped in my seat the first time I saw it happen, but within a few weeks, I hardly noticed his outbursts at all.

Wendy, a fifth-grader, was skinny, with frizzy, flame-red hair and skin as white as notebook paper. She looked like a walking matchstick in black-and-white saddle shoes. She would wet her pants on occasion, and the odor would circulate around the classroom. One at a time, we'd notice the smell and look to see the puddle on the floor at her feet. She'd fold her arms across her desk and put her head down to hide her face.

Then there was Hal, also a fifth-grader. He was as tall as our teacher and three times as wide. He wore black orthopedic shoes and walked in a flippy-floppy sort of way, like he was wearing scuba fins at the beach. He rarely said a word to anyone, but he became my best buddy at school.

Lunchtime was humiliating. Led by our teacher, we walked single file down the gravel path. It was a precisely orchestrated affair. We marched liked hungry misfits — the daily parade of retards. *Crunch, crunch, crunching* our way to the main building and into the cafeteria inside, where we sat in our assigned seats at a table designated by a sign — *Special Education Only*.

Without fail, one of us would do something to show how different we were from the rest of the children. One day, Wendy jumped from her seat and ran for the girl's bathroom while holding her dress tightly between her legs. Everyone roared with laughter, except for us — her classmates. Stanley had several outbursts in the lunchroom. Everyone would stop and stare at him, but we kept eating our fish sticks and bologna sandwiches. A school bully walked by our table one day. He reached over Hal's shoulder and swept his lunch tray onto the floor, then said, "Whatcha gonna do about that, fatso!"

Hal didn't move a muscle, but I jumped up and tackled the slimy, no-good butthead. I knocked him to the ground and began punching him in the face. We tussled back and forth on the floor and eventually knocked over a table. Food went flying. A lunch aide sent the bully and me to the principal's office. My parents were called in for a meeting with the school administrator. Just like before, Mom sobbed, and my father seethed. I was suspended from Special Education. The doctors increased my meds.

Shortly following my fight at school, the final episode of abuse with Gene Lang happened. When it did, something inside of me completely shattered. I lost my boyhood energy and drifted into a broken, compliant fog. I did schoolwork in class and spent the rest of the day in my room at home, drawing pictures of football and baseball players, and my favorite motorcycles or cars.

Writing this now, I feel bad for not remembering more about my classmates. None of them should be forgotten. Our differences disappeared in the understanding eyes of our shared experience. We found belonging as we endured the painful experience of being outcast together.

Stanley noticed how terrible I was at math and helped me with my equations without a hint of superiority. And Wendy had eyes that glowed blue like sapphires. I would sit in my seat and stare at her from across the room. On the rare occasion she looked back, I felt butterflies in my stomach and had to look away. Hal and I sat side by side in summer school. We talked when he was in the mood to talk.

I choose to believe Stan, and Wendy, Hal, and I were all doing the best we knew how to do. I even believe the same about the children who made fun of us and the adults who treated us poorly. I realize now they didn't understand the hurt they were inflicting or how they could do better.

Shame is a profound feeling of worthlessness. We all suffer from it here and there, no matter how hard we try to escape it. Yet when we face our shame, and admit it to someone who will understand, we are catapulted into the frontier of authentic, compassionate relationships.

MY OFFICE LOOKS OUT over a grassy field where neighborhood boys gather after school. I often keep the window open because I enjoy the raucous sounds they make with their horseplay. I'll stop my work sometimes and lean back in my chair to listen and reminisce.

I remembered sitting in the converted trailer classroom with Hal and my other classmates. I was a towheaded blond, four-and-a-half feet tall and about eighty pounds. I wore my favorite striped T-shirt with ketchup stains down the front and blue jeans with holes in the knees. My canvas high-tops were muddy. My head was down as I held a pencil in hand; my fingernails were caked with dirt. It looked like I was doing my schoolwork, but I was likely daydreaming about life outside the black, painted-over windows.

I daydreamed a lot in school — no surprise, I guess — and yet often I was praying while doing it. My prayers were not formal, well-mannered prayers like the ones in church. No, not at all. My prayers were quiet whimpers of desperation. I promised God that I would never look at my father's porn again and that I would stop sneaking his cigarettes to smoke behind the garage. I begged to be forgiven for the countless lies I had told and all the promises to be good I had broken.

Silence was all I ever heard in return. No one seemed to pay attention. Until one day, I was finally given the gift of unexpected change and adventure.

Early in the summer after fifth grade, my father rented out our Sandpiper Street home and put most of our furniture into storage. My father had been working on completing his PhD from the University of Colorado in Boulder. He took a sabbatical from the university, and our family moved to Boulder to fulfill the residency requirement for his degree.

Mom's Uncle Pahr had once lived in Boulder. He still owned his house there and offered it to us. I thought Uncle Pahr was an amazing man. He had survived World War I without severe injury and had become a successful farmer back home in Kansas. He suffered a different kind of wound, my mother told me. A hometown girl had rejected his love for her, so he never married. After years of loneliness on the farm, he moved to Boulder for a fresh start. He built his house on Pleasant Street, at the foot of Flagstaff Mountain.

His house was a simple rectangle — about twelve feet by fifty feet. When we arrived, my father set up partitions in the room at the front of the house, so my sister and I had our own places to sleep. My spot was barely big enough for a small bed, with just enough floor space to stand and turn around. I kept my clothes in cardboard boxes under the bed. My dog Whitey slept on the floor beside me. It became known as my "cubby hole." Whenever my father was irritated with me, he'd say sternly, "You need to go back to your cubby hole."

My father began his work in earnest and drove to Denver twice a week to play the organ at a church there. He was rarely at home. My mother, sister, and I attended a small church in Boulder where people shared potluck suppers and the great outdoors. Mom took a job in a bank and was happier than I'd ever known her to be. She enrolled my sister at the junior high and me at Flatirons Elementary. I was relieved when she didn't tell the school about the doctor's diagnosis, the medications I had taken, or the two years I spent in the retard trailer. I learned I was less likely to act stupid or bad when I was around people who didn't assume I was that way.

My father said team sports were out of the question because the field was too far away and the fees were too expensive. So I spent the summer tramping around the woods of Flagstaff Mountain, with Whitey tagging along. Whitey and I also explored the city of Boulder. We often stopped at Chautauqua Park, where we would hike up and down the Flatirons. These massive rock formations look like God had set his iron down against the mountain when he was finished pressing his pants. By the time we arrived at the top, I was drenched with sweat, and Whitey's tongue was hanging out the side of his mouth. The climb was always worth the effort. You could almost see the Nebraska state line from up there.

One day I noticed a boy about my same age delivering newspapers. The next afternoon, my mother stood behind me at the front desk of the Boulder Daily Camera newspaper while I filled out an application. They hired me, and after two weeks of training, I delivered newspapers to forty homes after school each day and on Saturday and Sunday mornings. Always eager to follow, Whitey ran alongside as I rode my bicycle on my route.

I was eleven years old and there was a local fishing pond nearby. I wanted to be a fisherman again. I used my newspaper earnings to replace my Zebco and the other fishing gear I had lost three years before on that horrible day with Gene Lang. I also made enough money to buy a minibike from Sears, which I rode up and down the twisty road to the top of Flagstaff. On occasion, the police stopped me and asked for my license, which of course, they knew I didn't have. They'd let me off each time with a stern warning to ride it only on dirt trails and never on paved streets until I was properly licensed.

"Absolutely, sir. Never again. I promise!"

This happened repeatedly. Each time they would make me push my minibike home, following me in their patrol car while shaking their heads and chuckling the whole way.

I began the sixth grade just like every other sixth-grader at Flatirons Elementary. The tall classroom windows were floor to ceiling like I'd never seen before. As I sat in class, I stared outside, watching the trees moving in the wind or the rain or snow falling. My classmates and I sat at tables, three or four of us working together in groups.

I liked a girl in the class named Denise, and she liked me too. She went skiing with her family on winter weekends and returned on Mondays with her face tanned golden brown, except where her ski goggles covered her eyes. I couldn't help but stare — she had raccoon eyes in reverse. I sometimes imagined Denise and me getting married. We would live on the backside of the mountain where we could see the best sunsets, and we'd have three or four reasonably well-behaved kids. Denise would drive them to school and run her errands in a red Corvette. I would drive a lifted four-wheel-drive pickup to my job as a police officer, firefighter, or maybe a lieutenant colonel in the Army.

At Christmas time, I used my paper route money to buy an album for my sister, an electric can opener for Mom, and wool-lined leather gloves for my father, to protect his hands from the cold. It was a mild winter that year. One warmer than usual Sunday afternoon, Whitey and I were heading up a steep trail on Flagstaff when suddenly he dashed into the bushes. Without a second thought, I chased after him. We burst into a small clearing and came face-to-face with the biggest skunk I had ever seen and three babies cowering behind her. Whitey and I had encountered raccoons, snakes, coyotes, deer, and other skunks on previous hikes up the mountain. He always had enough sense to keep his distance, but here we were, face-to-face with an angry mother skunk just a few feet away. We stood there frozen in place, sizing each other up. It was a skunky standoff.

Then the mama skunk began to stamp her feet and snort like an angry mother bear. Whitey growled back and bared his teeth. The hair along his spine stood like porcupine quills from his neck to his tail. When he lunged at one of the babies, the mama skunk whirled around and gave him a big squirt to the snout. I lunged to grab Whitey, and got a good spray too. Covered in horrifically pungent skunk spray, I turned and ran down the mountain as fast as I could, with Whitey close behind. We ran back to Pleasant Street and straight to the side of our house, where I rinsed my face with the garden hose and began hosing down Whitey. He stood there stiff-legged and shaking, glaring at me like it was all my fault.

Mom heard the commotion. She came outside and had me strip to my skivvies right there outside the back door. Then she marched me into the bathroom and left me to soak in the tub while she went to buy as much tomato juice as she could find. Our neighbor was a self-proclaimed expert in skunk deodorizing. He swore the tomato juice would take the smell away, but it didn't. Whitey and I slept in a tent behind the house the next two nights, and no one sat next to me at school the whole week. Not even Denise.

Vesta, along with my father's sister and brother and their families, visited early in the spring. It was a multiday gathering with far too many people crammed into our tiny house. Mom took time off from her job to play host, but I could tell she walked on eggshells around Vesta. Within a few days, she had given up trying to play host. Her sadness returned, as did her old pattern of sleeping most of the day.

One afternoon amidst the noise and family chatter, no one noticed when Whitey snuck out of the yard. Later that evening, the phone rang. It was an officer from the Boulder Police. He asked for me by name. Whitey had been run over by a car and killed a few blocks away, in front of the home of one of my paper route customers. She recognized him as the dog who ran beside me when I tossed her paper onto her porch. The officer knew where I lived because of my minibike. I recognized him when he knocked on our door a few minutes later. "I'm so sorry, little buddy," he said. "Losing a dog is the worst kind of thing. I thought you might want to have this."

He handed me Whitey's collar and tag, shook my hand, then turned to walk back to his patrol car. I stood on the front porch for a moment, holding Whitey's collar and tag. The sun was almost gone, and the air was getting cool. Mom had gone to bed. My father and everyone else were crammed shoulder to shoulder in the kitchen, eating supper. I slipped through them unnoticed. I went to my cubby hole, where I sobbed alone. Only a few feet away, my father and his family didn't miss a beat. They just kept eating their dinner.

I REVISITED BOULDER THIS PAST FALL. I had been back many times, but as it has been fifty years since living there, and I was in the process of writing this book, I felt more purpose with this visit than the ones before.

I drove to Chautauqua Park before sunrise. Found a flat rock, sat down huddled inside my jacket, and waited for the sun to light up the Flatirons. A group of young men walked by me in the dark for an early morning hike, their headlamps illuminating the path at their feet and their breath into a steamy glow. One of them had his dog walking alongside. He was last in line and gave me a friendly nod as he passed, like each of them had before. I envied their youth and the experience they were about to share. I started to ask if I could join them, but I didn't because I wondered if I could keep up. The quick confidence of my youth was long gone. That, and when I saw the young man's dog, I thought of Whitey, which brought a sting of emotion I might not be able to hide.

Once the sun had warmed the air a little, I drove up the steep, twisty road to the top of Flagstaff. From there I looked west to view the higher range of mountains. Snow was already building on their peaks. Then I looked east over the city to the farm country beyond. I could look down and see Uncle

Pahr's old house on Pleasant Street and Flatirons Elementary three blocks away. Afterward, I drove by his old house, then to my old school. It was closed because of Covid-19, but a school employee allowed me to walk the grounds around the building. I strolled the field where I had played softball and kickball. I walked around the playground admiring the new equipment that stood where a rusty swing set and monkey bars made of galvanized pipe had been. I remembered how my sweaty playground hands stuck to the cold steel on winter days. I even found the secret place where Denise and I practiced our kissing.

Lastly, I drove around the neighborhood, retracing my paper route. I stopped in front of the house where Whitey died. As I sat in the car, I remembered Whitey never learned to fetch a ball, so I sometimes thought he was a stupid, retarded dog. Maybe that's why I loved him so much. He did know every stop on my paper route and often ran ahead to lead the way. At night, once he had finished licking his dog bowl clean, he would lie on the floor next to me in my cubby hole. I would reach my arm off the side of the bed and rub his ears as we drifted off to sleep.

For a moment, I wondered if it would have been better if the officer had brought me Whitey's lifeless body, not just his collar and tag. Looking back, I wish I could have buried Whitey in a place on Flagstaff Mountain where we had roamed together.

Grief is obnoxious in how it comes and goes. It shows up without notice and makes itself at home as if it owns me. I always feel embarrassed at the mess I am, but grief is messy too.

Grief's messy intrusions reconnect me with what I have loved the most.

ONCE MY FATHER COMPLETED HIS STUDIES, our life on Pleasant Street in Boulder was packed away as a memory, and we returned to Houston. My father resumed teaching at the university and playing the organ at the big church again. The ugly sounds from my parents' bedroom returned, creeping through the wall at night worse than before. His porn returned, hidden in the same places.

However, some things had changed. Folks at church now greeted my father with a reverent, "Hello, *Dr. Zailer.*"

He responded with a polite nod and smile. "Oh please, just call me Lew."

I reclaimed my place on the baseball field, and Daniel invited me back to play on his football team with the older boys. I came back from Boulder bigger, stronger, and with more confidence. I was quick to show everyone that I could dish it out as good or better than they could to me. I even stopped sneaking my father's cigarettes. I was thirteen now, so I bought them for myself.

When I started the seventh grade, I earned a spot on the junior high school football team. The starting fullback — a ninth-grader — was a jerk, and we were soon caught up in a one-on-one personal competition. One day after practice, it escalated into pushing and shoving in the locker room. He pushed me to the floor backward, but I stood up, grabbed his helmet, and smashed him three times in the head. I thought it was a great way to end the conflict, but the coaches didn't see it that way. They kicked me off the team.

The following day I was pulled out of class and suspended from school. My parents were called to come to get me, but no one came. I sat in the office until the end of the school day, when I was finally sent home. When I arrived, Mom was in bed asleep. My father was practicing for a recital.

This was the first of many junior high suspensions. Notices for each suspension were sent home with me, along with requests for parent-teacher conferences. I would set each notice on the kitchen counter, but my parents rarely mentioned them. If my parents said anything about the notice, I would stay home watching television until the suspension lifted. If they said nothing about it, I would pretend to go to school as usual but aimlessly ride my bike around town. I passed rows and rows of small businesses, like used car lots, bars, massage parlors, barbershops, pawnshops, and automotive repair shops, until it was time to go home.

One day when I was on suspension, I stopped at a hamburger stand called The Purple Cow. It was sandwiched between a pawn shop and a used car lot. I filled out an application and was hired for an after-school job. They gave me a crisp white shirt and a soda jerk hat as a uniform. The smiling face of a purple cow was printed on each of them. The drive-thru customers spoke their order into a gargantuan fiberglass cow that was painted — yes, you guessed it — purple. The owner was grumpy except when he was drinking. Thank goodness he kept a bottle in his desk drawer. When the shop closed at nine, I wiped down the tables and booths, then mopped the floors with hot water and bleach. Then I would pedal my way home happy and proud, having earned a dollar an hour.

One afternoon, my boss had me deliver burgers to the pawnshop next door. When I opened the door, I stood in awe at what I saw. The store was crammed floor to ceiling with men's and women's clothes, overcoats, handbags, guitars, amplifiers, violins, drum kits, saxophones, sports equipment, rifles, shotguns, and camping gear. It was a fantasy land of exotic bargains courtesy of someone else's misfortune.

I walked to the back of the store to hand the manager the bag of burgers. He stood behind a long glass display case. It had knives and handguns to the right, with watches and jewelry to the left. A small multicolored pendant that looked like one of the crown jewels caught my eye. I moved to get a closer look.

"You like that?" asked the manager.

"Yes, sir. What is it?"

"That, my fine young friend, is a certified master-crafted opal mosaic. A rare and wonderous gem that is sure to impress the most discriminating investor. Could you ever possibly afford something so exotic?"

He pulled the pendant from the case and set it on the top glass to further entice me. My eyes grew wide in its glory. The opal was the size of a nickel. Mashed inside the pendent were colors of blue, green, orange, yellow, and red. All the colors together sparkled in a way that made each of them stand out more brightly. The label described exactly what the man had just said. *Master-Crafted Opal Mosaic.*

"Look at this here, young man. It comes complete with a certificate of authenticity and a genuine simulated gold necklace."

Christmas was coming. It would make a perfect gift for Mom. It was also thirty-five dollars — more than two week's pay.

I looked at the manager and said, "I'll be back."

At the end of the week, I returned with my paycheck in hand, planning to put it on layaway. The manager had a better plan. He discounted the price in half and had me sign my check over as payment in full. He handed me the certified master-crafted opal mosaic, winked at me, then said, "Get out of here, you little stinker. I'll grow broke doing business with the likes of you."

In junior high, there were two things that I wanted badly: money and a car. I squirreled away my earnings like nuts for winter, hiding it in a can in my bedroom closet until Mom found it and took me to the bank to open an account. At fifteen, I received my provisional driver's license and bought my first car: a faded red tugboat on wheels — better known as a *Chevy Impala.*

I kept the Chevy for a few months, sold it for a hundred-dollar profit, and set my sights on a shiny red Mercury Cougar. I got my regular license the day I turned sixteen — three days after starting high school — and bought the Cougar the very next day. I started driving myself to school, work, and church, separately from my family, to avoid the drama.

Mom sometimes rode along with me. One warm Sunday night, she and I were driving home from church. I still remember the freeway streetlights reflecting off the shiny hood of the Cougar as we passed them one by one. Everything was quiet except for the hum of the engine and the rhythmic sound of the tires on the pavement.

Mom broke the silence. "Did Gene Lang ever do anything bad to you?"

My heart nearly stopped. Panic hit me like a wave. I said nothing at first, pretending like I hadn't heard. When she started to ask again, I launched at her in anger, yelling at her like I'd heard my father do countless times before. I even felt my face turn a burning red like his.

"There you go again, making up stupid, insane things out of thin air! You're crazy! You're sick! Why do you have to be so paranoid?!"

Mom cowered against the passenger door and didn't say another word the rest of the way home. She jumped out of the car the moment we arrived and went inside — I'm sure to take a pill, because that's what she did when my father yelled at her. She went straight to bed.

That night I tossed and turned with the raging shame of being my father's son.

I LEFT THE SCHOOL suspensions behind in junior high, but my poor grades followed me in high school. My grades were so bad, the high school guidance counselor had me take an aptitude test to determine what career would suit me best. The results suggested I should become a mechanic of some kind or do building maintenance. Following that guidance, I enrolled in a program where I went to school in the morning and worked to get job training in the afternoon.

My first job was in a warehouse for a company that repaired sewage pumps. I disassembled and cleaned the broken pumps so the trained mechanics could rebuild them. These were sewage pumps, and they came to my workstation full of *you know what*. Many were so old the cast iron parts were fused together by corrosion. I learned to use pneumatic impact wrenches, propane torches, electric chipping hammers, and grinders to get the pumps apart without damaging them beyond repair, or losing a finger in the process. I would scrape the sludge out, wash the parts with a solvent and sanitizer, and then rinse everything with a high-pressure hose. Then I used a shovel and broom to move the smelly brown waste to an underground septic tank, where it was later pumped into a tanker truck and hauled away.

It wasn't long before the smell was too much for me, so I quit and went to work on a maintenance crew in an office building. When the building was sold a few months later, I was left without a job. At that point I decided my career needed an upgrade, so I went to work selling shoes in a department store. I dressed in a suit and tie and always kept my shoes buffed to a perfect shine.

Several times when I was in high school, my mother spiraled down in her depression and she became disoriented to her surroundings. For her, life with my father was an ever-present threat, filled with unrelenting fear. She was hopelessly alone, wandering in the dark despair that she must have felt would never change. Afraid of what she might do, I would follow her around the house, watching her argue with people who were not there. It was a mystery who these people were. She would walk in circles throughout the house, double-checking every door and window to make sure they were locked. I would follow her, trying to have a conversation with her, trying to keep her safe. My father was unconcerned when she acted this way. He spent his time practicing his music or reading his Latin-translation Bible. However, when she finally grew intolerable to him, he put her in the car and drove her to a hospital across town. The doctors sedated her and locked her away for months at a time.

While my father was generally unfazed by my mother's illness, other things stressed him to the breaking point. By this time, my sister was away at college, studying music.

I remember him pacing back and forth in the house, worrying about how to pay for her tuition and board. He would only stop his pacing to sneak outside for a smoke. Smoking was his best-kept secret, but we all knew and just pretended that we didn't. *It was always better not to embarrass him.*

To add to my father's stress, he was fired from the university a few months before making tenure. He told me it was terribly unjust and said, "I'm gonna sue them all!"

His name had been whispered in rumors of a salacious scandal. I never knew exactly what was said, but the gossip was that someone on the university's music staff had been sexually involved with a student. I only know that my father never sued anyone but went away quietly instead. He also quit the big church downtown, taking his talents to a smaller church on the city's west side.

Near the end of eleventh grade, my English teacher told me to plan to attend summer school because I was flunking. Again! This wasn't eleventh-grade English, but tenth-grade English, which I had already flunked twice before. I walked out of high school that day and never went back. For weeks I waited and hoped my parents, or someone from school or church, would talk with me to change my mind. No one ever did. Though I understood the overwhelming nature of my mother's illness, I had to admit how hurt I was that she did nothing to encourage me to stay in school. I was betrayed by my mother, and of course, by my father too. The abandonment I felt seemed complete.

My best option was to return to the sewage pump warehouse and ask for my job back. Four dollars an hour was a nice sum for a high school dropout back in the day. I promised the manager I would be the best sewage pump cleaner in the history of sewage pump cleaners. He rehired me, and I started back full-time the next day.

A few weeks later, I took an evening job at a community recreation center. I handed out sports equipment, coached kids' basketball, gave racquetball instruction, and learned to play the game myself, then locked the building at ten o'clock every night. I felt like things were falling into place for me until the day the rec center director called me into his office at the start of my shift. He told me that customers and staff had been complaining about the way I smelled. I told him what I did during the day and explained I always wore a shop apron with rubber boots and gloves at the warehouse. And I always showered and dressed in fresh clothes before coming to the rec center. I guess the smell had damaged my nostrils. I also then knew why the other staff never invited me for burgers and shakes after work. I had been wearing cow-patty cologne and never knew it.

Thank God for the director. He offered me a full-time job so I could stop shoveling poo.

FOR THE NEXT TWO YEARS, from the time I was eighteen until twenty, I played racquetball at the rec center most every morning before working my shift in the afternoon. I got good enough to play in local tournaments on Saturdays. On Sundays, I would sit with my mom at the new church. My father sat at the organ and lingered there after the service, chatting with the choir members. I would stand beside Mom while she waited for him. People stopped by to say hello to us. They always mentioned what a great blessing my father was to the church and to God. The way they talked of God made him sound like a celestial genie who granted *your-every-wish* if you were one of the people who pleased him. They would ask me the same question every week as if it had been a thousand years since they saw me the week before. "Well, hello, David. Wonderful to see you. What are you doing with your life these days?"

I smiled back, shook their hands firmly, and then lied, telling them I was heading to college soon. What I wanted to do was crawl under a pew and hide.

At the racquetball tournaments, I met players from all over the country. They told me San Diego, California, was the place to be if I was serious about racquetball. A sales representative from a sports equipment company in San Diego heard of my dedication. He offered me equipment, clothing, and to pay my travel expenses if I moved there. Intrigued by the opportunity, I gave my notice and withdrew every dime I had in the bank. I packed only the essentials. Socks and underwear. An extra pair of jeans and my freshly polished boots. Every T-shirt I owned and two dress shirts. I took the pillow off my bed and an old quilt my grandmother had made back in Cheyenne. And of course, I couldn't forget to take the Bible Mom had recently bought for me, like she did every year.

By this time, I was driving an old silver Mercury, whose color had faded to a sunbaked gray. I called it the Gray Ghost. The radiator leaked, and it burned oil so bad it blew gray smoke out the tailpipe. It hardly went sixty on the freeway, but it started and got me from one place to the other. At the ripe old age of twenty, I packed the Gray Ghost and headed west to San Diego.

I left Houston in late August and drove twelve hours a day for two and a half days. *Fifteen hundred sweltering miles.* At night, I slept in the back seat along the side of the road.

I found a one-room apartment in San Diego. In the parking lot next to a dumpster, I found apple crates to sit on. I bought a swimming pool float for a bed and used my grandmother's quilt for bedding. Within a week, I had a job at a gym popular with the best racquetball players in town. The guys adopted me into their local family by beating me without mercy game after game, day after day. I played until midday, then I would lift weights or run on the beach till early afternoon. My body grew stronger and filled out. My skin turned golden brown. My hair went blonde. I found great joy in the process of training and competing. The more I worked at it, the more joy grew inside, the more confident I became, and the better I played.

After training each day, I worked at the gym from four to eleven in the evening. I spent weekends at the beach with friends I met at the gym. We often stayed late enough to watch the sunset burning into the ocean while eating fish tacos slathered with Baja sauce.

One of my new friends invited me to church with him on a Saturday night. Church had become a complicated experience for me. On the one hand, it felt ill-fitting and seemed irrelevant. On the other hand, I grew up indoctrinated with the belief that good people went to church. I felt emotionally indentured to attend.

If you want to be a good person, you had better go to church. Right?

My friend's church was completely different than the churches I attended back in Houston. First of all, nobody wore double-knit suits. Everyone wore denim or corduroy and cotton. There was no organ or choir. A team of singers led the music, accompanied by a band playing electric guitars, bass, and drums. They stood center stage under spotlights with perfect sun-kissed hair, tan skin, and bright movie-star teeth. They raised their hands as they sang and swayed hypnotically to the music.

The preacher wore a Hawaiian shirt, faded blue jeans, and sandals. His hair was bleached blonde and hung down past his shoulders like a rock star. He held a black leather Bible against his chest while strutting back and forth across the stage. He was a Rockstar Preacher preaching to his adoring church fans!

He told the story of how he had once been a teenage drug addict living on the streets of San Diego, but at nineteen, he heard a holy calling from God. It was a message instructing him to go to Bible college to be trained in godliness. By twenty-two, his dedication had been richly rewarded with a beautiful wife, two beautiful children, and a loyal flock of sheep.

Every week the Rockstar Preacher mentioned *the burden* of speaking to us by the thousands, imploring us to save the evil world all around us. He was a powerhouse religious Rockstar. The young ladies sat starry-eyed. The packed auditorium was spellbound and caught in the rapture of religious ecstasy — including me.

AFTER THREE YEARS of hard competition, when I was twenty-three, I got injured. My sponsor declined to renew my sponsorship contract. I was working at the sports club and evaluating my future when I ran into a man I had met at the Rockstar church. He was a prominent leader there and never shy to challenge people to "leave your sins behind and sacrifice your life to please God."

That morning, he had a couple of questions for me.

"David, are you going to play games the rest of your life?" he asked. "Are you going to waste the only little life God will ever give you?"

I always had a secret fear deep inside that my life would end up in the toilet. I also had limited my options by quitting school. Nevertheless, I was a compulsive people-pleaser and felt I needed to prove my worth to God. The words of the Rockstar Preacher haunted me.

"Stop pleasing yourself and do something important to please God!"

After the man from the Rockstar church confronted me, I decided to enroll in Bible college. It seemed like the right way to atone for my lazy and stupid life.

The Bible classes were in the evening, so I quit the health club and went to work for a swimming pool construction company. I raced home after work each day for a shower and to get to class by six. I studied the history of the Old Testament, New Testament history, and the history of the early Christian church. The classes were terribly dull, but it was a sacrifice I was willing to make for the chance to be important and impress others. Maybe I could even please God?

My classmates were mostly older men who were following their own "holy calling." That was how most of them explained it. Four of them were from the Rockstar church. Guess how they dressed? They wore Hawaiian shirts, blue jeans, and sandals. They carried their black Bibles under their arms the same way the Rockstar Preacher did. Three of them had even grown their gray hair down past their slumping shoulders. When I arrived late or came straight from work muddy and sweaty, I noticed they would give me the sideways stink eye. I thought they looked like a scroungy, flea-bitten litter of gray-haired pot-bellied Rockstar Preacher pups, born behind the dumpster of a religious junkyard.

Not that I was ever judgmental or bitter.

One evening as I was leaving class, the class instructor directed me to the school administrator's office. He was at his desk waiting for me.

Without even saying hello, he asked, "Have you been smoking cigarettes?"

Confession time. I had always been smoking ever since sneaking my father's cigarettes back when I was eight. It was never a lot, and I kept it secret. *Of course I kept it secret!* Imagine if my racquetball sponsor or my competitors found out. It certainly wasn't something we talked about between running wind sprints in the sand on the beach. I wasn't dumb enough to tell anybody at the Rockstar church. I usually kept mints or gum in my mouth, so no one ever said anything. Nevertheless, here I was, faced with a straight-up question. *Tell the truth, or tell a lie.*

"Yes, sir. I smoke and have for some time. Not much, maybe three or four a day."

With that, the administrator stepped out of his office but then came back quickly with two of the class instructors and said, "We're going to give you some help on this."

They put their hands on my shoulders — one even put his hand on the top of my head. The administrator began to pray. And man oh man, it was nuclear-powered prayer. As good a prayer as I had ever heard. Loud with emotional beseeching for healing and deliverance. A prayer bona fide with lots of "thees" and "thous."

I felt their hands squeezing and relaxing as each man quietly whispered along.

"Yes, Jesus. I agree. Yes, Jesus. I agree."

The administrator concluded the prayer with a thunderous crescendo: "AMEN!"

Then the men invited me to stand with them. They vigorously shook my hand, patted me on the shoulder, congratulating me on experiencing God's deliverance and my newfound freedom. You know what? It worked! I felt delivered and healed when I walked out of Bible college that night. I joyously threw the cigs away in a trash can just outside the building and didn't have a single craving for three days.

Woo-hoo! Victory! Like a caged bird set loose, I was free — PRAISE GOD!!!

Then came the fourth day. That's when I heard the sneaky little thought that almost every cigarette smoker who has ever tried to quit knows miserably well.

C'mon, man — just one. Then I promise I'll never bother you again. I promise.

The craving to smoke was relentless. I finally caved. By day six, I was smoking just like before. One at lunch. One after work. One as I drove home in the evening. This time the smoking made me feel weaker and more ashamed than ever. I was doubly careful not to be seen by anyone I knew. A few months later, the administrator called me back into his office.

"Have you still been smoking?"

I remembered how the prayer had helped me and assumed I could get a booster shot.

"Yes, sir. Only a couple a day."

He showed me a paper that I had signed when I enrolled. It was a pledge. I had pledged not to drink alcohol or smoke cigarettes or behave in any manner that would stain the reputation of Jesus or the church I was training to serve. I didn't know what to say, but he knew what to say to me. He booted me out of Bible college.

AFTER I WAS KICKED OUT OF BIBLE COLLEGE, the best thing I knew was to work hard for the pool company and learn everything I could. I ran a jackhammer on an excavation crew. I dug trenches for the technicians who installed the plumbing and electrical systems. I watched the experts and learned how to measure, cut, fit the pipes together and make safe electrical connections. I learned to read plans and tie steel rebar. I installed solar panels, learned to set coping, tile, and to finish concrete. To further impress my bosses, I traded in the Grey Ghost for a used pickup. I even bought tools with the bit of money left over each month after my rent and truck payment.

I found a new church to attend and met new friends there. They were primarily guys like me who worked in the trades. One evening after work, we met for pizza. Along with pizza, they ordered a pitcher of beer to split between them. I ordered a glass of soda. At the end of the evening, my soda glass was empty, so I washed down the rest of my pizza with the small amount of beer left in the pitcher.

Almost instantly, that small amount of beer washed away the constant feeling of hopeless struggle that had haunted me since childhood. It was gone, I tell ya! I felt deliverance! Freedom!

It was winter, and as we walked outside, my friends reached for their jackets. I felt toasty warm.

Wow, that's why people drink that stuff, I thought to myself.

It tasted like bait bucket water from last week's fishing trip, but the effect was terrific. I felt taller, confident, handsome, charming, and intelligent. It was great until the moment that wonderful feeling began to disappear. Then all I could think about was getting it back again. Two weeks later, I got my buddies back together for more pizza. However, the pizza wasn't necessary once I realized I could get the same feeling with only beer.

That same winter, my buddies and I attended a social at the church. I was standing in the back drinking punch and watching people when a girl across the room caught my eye. I had seen her before. Her name was Janice. She saw me staring at her; our eyes locked like laser beams. She blushed. I moved across the room toward her in my most confident John Wayne swagger and mixed in a hint of John Travolta *Saturday Night Fever*. I didn't want to be too overwhelming; you know. As I was about to say hello, an invisible foot-grabbing demon reached out of the carpet and tripped me. I landed face-first in her lap. It was love at first face-plant.

Soon, Janice and I were a thing. We spent every moment together we could. On Saturdays, we drove up to Julian in the mountains east of San Diego. We took walks along the beach on Sundays after church. At our dinners in La Jolla, she had a glass of wine, and I had a beer. She told me I was the godly man she had been praying for. I told her I loved her and worked extra hours to save up for an engagement ring. I had always wanted another dog since Whitey had been killed, so we got a dog and named him DJ. D after my name, J after Janice.

Unfortunately, my obsession with alcohol was becoming a real problem. In honesty, it was never only about alcohol. I never learned to like the taste, but I always loved the feeling it gave me. My problem was the relentless obsession to regain the euphoric feeling I felt with that first beer. Whenever I was with Janice, all I could think about was beer. I was equally concerned about hiding it so she wouldn't know I had a problem.

I struggled secretly for months before I finally broke down and told her about my drinking. She was alarmed and I promised to stop. However, stopping was not my problem; I could do that. Not starting again; *that* was my problem.

Over the next year, she became ever more troubled by the promises I failed to keep. I should not have been surprised when she broke up with me. Her last words to me were, "I'm sorry I ever met you."

The contempt of those words lingered on me like the smell from the sewage pumps.

The wheels fell off my cart in the first year after our breakup. I drank more, and I drank more often. I always made it to work on time, but my hands would sometimes shake in the morning. Sometimes I vomited or peed on myself in my sleep at night. A friend I confided in suggested I might be an alcoholic and told me to go to the church for help.

The counselor there told me I was too young to be an alcoholic. He told me my real problem was my sin and spiritual rebellion. His answer? To read the Bible and pray — of course, what else! He said I needed to be sincere in repenting of my selfish ways. I did my best to be sincere and follow his guidance, but I was drinking again in less than a week.

At twenty-five, and a miserable year after our breakup, I packed my tools and belongings into my truck with my dog, and I headed east across the desert for Houston.

DJ's tail was wagging. Mine was between my legs.

I returned to my old room at my parents' house. The air conditioner still made the same *ka-clank* sound. Every day I noticed the scar on the side of the tree. I looked for a job in the mornings and took DJ to the sports park in the afternoons, where we jogged around the baseball field, and I tossed a tennis ball for him to chase. I went to church on Sundays and sat with Mom as usual. The same people stopped after the service to say hello, and to ask what they always asked. "So nice to see you. What are you doing with your life these days?"

I would smile and shake their hands like I always had, then told them my pithy little lies about the great future ahead of me. In hindsight, I think it was quite an accomplishment that I never punched anyone in the face. My father was more than happy to tell others about the sad details of my life. "Some girl in California broke his poor little heart, so he came running back home."

Late one morning after a job interview, I stopped by a 7-Eleven store for a soda but walked out with a six-pack of Lone Star beer. Why? It made no sense other than I was an alcoholic who valued a good buy on beer. I drove to the sports park and sat in my truck at the baseball field to have just one or two, but I drank all six. It was well after dinner before I went home that night. My father was sitting on the couch reading his favorite Greek-language New Testament. I didn't hold back and told him, "I think I might be an alcoholic, and I don't know what to —"

I didn't get in one more word before he jumped up off the couch in a tirade.

"I knew you would do something like this. Why do you have to embarrass me? Don't you ever, ever tell anyone about this. Just stop it. I don't want to hear about it again!"

He stormed down the hallway to his bedroom, slamming the door behind him. The beer buzz was instantly gone. I slumped on the couch where he had been lying and stared at the wall across the room.

Mom appeared in the doorway a few minutes later. She was dressed in her faded pink bathrobe and dirty, worn fluffy slippers. She sat down next to me without saying a word and began to pat my knee with her hand gently. Her face looked waxed over with the sweaty residue from the pills in her system. Her skin often appeared like that. I could smell the pungent odor of the chemicals weeping through the pores of her skin, but I didn't care. I reached out and put my arm around her shoulder. She leaned close and looked up at me, and then smiled. After a moment, I smiled back.

My mother knew a lot about suffering.

At that simple, quiet moment, she put her suffering to beautiful use by making it present to me as a gift, so I was not alone with mine.

Sitting with her, the anger and disappointment I had long felt because of her incapacitating sickness was wiped away. I stopped needing her to be anything more than who she already was.

I HEARD ABOUT A JOB OPENING with a swimming pool company in Austin and drove there to interview. They hired me, and I found a room to rent nearby. The homeowner was a wonderful Texas gent named Graham. His house had a nice-sized backyard, and he also had a dog, so he was happy to have DJ. Graham and I became good friends.

Most days after work, DJ and I went running around the lake at the center of town. On Saturdays, I did side jobs for extra money. On any off days and many Sunday afternoons, I would drive around exploring the hill country of central Texas with DJ riding shotgun. With his head out the window and ears flapping in the wind, I found I liked the area and began saving to buy a house for me and the future Mrs. I always assumed I'd get married.

On Saturday nights, I polished up my boots and went to one of the local honkytonks for a beer or two — in other words, I got sloshed — and there I met Texas cuties who drank the way I did. They taught me how to two-step, boot-scoot, the electric slide, and more personal moves after closing time. What little innocence I had left went straight to H-E-double hockey sticks. Even so, you have to hand it to me: I still made it to church most every Sunday morning. If not still a little drunk, I was definitely hungover.

My side work prospered and became my full-time occupation within a year. Soon I had some money in the bank, a new Chevy truck loaded with tools, and several pairs of new boots with belts to match. While I thought about it every day, I never drank a drop during the week, keeping my *wayward ways* to Saturday nights. One Saturday night, for reasons I don't know, I decided to stay home. I was twenty-seven years old.

At two o'clock on Sunday morning, Graham knocked on my bedroom door to tell me I had a phone call. When I picked up the phone, my father said, "Your mother is dead."

Before I could think to ask a single question, he began to tell me in a hysterical voice about the horrible argument he had with my mom.

Now wait, I thought. *They haven't had a real argument in twenty years.*

Their arguments were one-sided verbal slashings, with my father cutting her to the core.

He frantically went on to tell me about how she had shot herself, how the paramedics had come, and then the police. He explained how the police had tested his hands for gunpowder residue. As if it were almost a forgotten detail, he told how the paramedics failed to save my mother's life. The coroner had loaded her body into a van and hauled it away. Last, he said the most horrible part of it all was being left there alone by himself.

In less than twenty minutes I had my black suit packed, along with other clothes and things I might need. At that time of night, the highway between Austin and Houston was darker than dark. You have to be very careful on that stretch because there are as many deer on the road as cars.

I have no idea what I was thinking about as I drove. I remember the radio was off because I needed quiet to sort things out. I'm dang sure I was smoking like a chimney the whole way. The sun was rising as I pulled up to the house a little before six in the morning. The scar on my father's tree was the first thing I noticed as I walked across the front yard. He answered the door, and without greeting me, he began talking as if we had never hung up the phone three hours earlier. In the same frantic way, he told me the preacher from church had come to sit with him but had just left to prepare for Sunday services. My father then reached for my sleeve and led me down the hallway to their bedroom.

Bloody bed linens had been thrown to a corner of the room in a heap. On the mattress was a crimson bloodstain the size of a beach ball. The blood had soaked through and onto the carpet, forming another bloodstain the size of a football. Plastic wrappers from the medical devices used to try to save my mom lay strewn across the room. I knew at that moment, this image of my mother's blood would be engrained in my mind forever.

I asked my father to tell me again what had happened. He repeated the same story as before. He and my mother had been arguing.

Uh-huh, I thought.

He said he left the house for a walk, which meant he went to grab a smoke to cool his anger like he always did. When he returned, he found her propped up in bed against the headboard. He said he spoke to her, but when she didn't respond, he reached over and touched her. That was when she fell onto the floor, and he saw her bleeding from a hole behind her right ear. Thinking she had somehow hit her head, he called 911.

When the paramedics arrived and began lifesaving efforts, they found a 22-caliber revolver on the floor under her body. The paramedics then called the police.

My father went on to tell me how the police had interviewed him for hours. They then took the gun and said they would write a report. He handed me the detective's business card like he was refusing to give me any more details and said, "You call him if you want to know anything more."

My father started to leave the room, but then he paused and turned back to me.

He blurted, "I never wanted to marry that woman."

The world stopped when I heard him say that. As if lost in a bad dream, I heard myself asking, *What in God's terrible world am I supposed to do with that?*

As I stood looking at the room littered with my mother's blood and death, I didn't know what to say to my father. I needed silence, but silence wasn't possible because my father would not stop talking.

"The wedding should have never happened, but she had already planned it all, and everything was in place. She had come so far to Germany. I was too embarrassed to back out at the last minute. You know, David, I think I can be proud of myself. Just before you got here, I was looking at myself in the mirror. I was thinking how strong I've been for staying married to that woman for thirty years. You know how she was."

With that, he began to leave the room but stopped in the doorway again like he had forgotten something. He turned to me once more. "I don't know what I'm going to do without sex, and just look at this mess!"

He emphatically pointed at the room with a shaking finger and then the bed.

"She leaves me to deal with all of this. She never cared about me. It's just like her, so selfish. What am I supposed to do with no sex? Did she even think about that? I can't handle this. You have to clean it up!"

He walked out of the room.

I cleaned up my mom's blood.

I CALLED THE DETECTIVE Monday morning. He was like Joe Friday from the old *Dragnet* television series in the 1960s. He gave me just the facts and nothing but the facts. He confirmed my mother's death was an apparent suicide and that my father had no part in it. Well, *not legally*, I thought. He also told me that Mom had purchased the gun herself and where she bought it. I went to the gun store and spoke with the manager. He was a mountain of a man with a .357 holstered on his belt. "Yes, I remember her," he said. "She said she wanted it for protection. She seemed like a sweet lady but a bit nervous, I'd say. Sorry for your loss."

My sister had graduated college and was married with a child. She arrived on Monday afternoon with her family in tow. My mother was buried on a Wednesday. In the difficult days leading up to it, I worked hard to care for my father and sister, and most importantly, for my mother's memory. I took care of the details with the funeral home, the church, and our relatives. To be sure things were in order, I went to the funeral home hours before the wake. I spent much of that time sitting beside my mom's body in her casket. I couldn't stand the thought of her being alone; she had enough of that when she was alive.

She was dressed in her favorite dress. Lavender silk. Around her neck hung the opal mosaic pendant I had bought her. I thought back to the Christmas morning she unwrapped it. She almost did backflips of joy by the Christmas tree. I had never felt a happier moment. She had nicer jewelry, but everyone knew the opal pendant was her favorite. I loved the compliments she got from the ladies at church.

"Oh, thank you!" she would say, beaming to the ladies. "It's a certified master-crafted opal mosaic. My son bought it for me."

Something I didn't realize until I revisited this memory to write this book: I didn't think to give the funeral home my mother's opal mosaic for burial. My father picked out her dress. He was the only person, other than me, who would think to include the pendant.

While I sat with Mom as she lay in her casket, I kissed her forehead and felt a tumultuous mix of emotions. Love, joy, gratitude, but also regret, guilt, and shame. I spoke to her and said, "I am so sorry for refusing to eat my vegetables as a boy and leaving the toilet seat up when I knew better. I am sorry for being a lousy student, getting into all those fights, and making you go to all those parent-teacher conferences. I am sorry for being impatient with you when you were at your sickest. I am sorry for not understanding the horror of your life with my father. I am sorry for not protecting you. I am sorry for going to California and leaving you alone in your torture. I am terribly sorry you won't meet the woman I hope to marry or the grandchildren I thought we would give you. I know you would have spoiled them rotten."

As I was speaking my heart to her, I had a crazy notion she might suddenly sit up in her casket and yell, "Surprise!"

I would have fallen to the floor in shock. She would have laughed herself silly at the marvelous joke she played on me. Once I picked myself up, I would have laughed myself silly right along with her, like she and Grandpa had laughed.

Except he had been feigning his death. My mother wasn't.

I returned to Austin the day after her funeral. It was late Thursday night when I arrived back home. I was exhausted. Graham was still awake, watching television.

"The dogs got out a few days ago," he said. "I went to the pound and found mine but I didn't see DJ there."

DJ could be sneaky in the way he could pull off his collar. He also had jumped the fence once or twice. I found him waiting on the front lawn to greet me when I drove into the driveway at the end of the day. This was a first. DJ had never run off before.

Our dogs were almost inseparable, and since Graham's dog had been at the pound, I was certain DJ would be there too. At eight o'clock the next morning, I walked into the front door at the dog pound with DJ's collar, his tag, and a picture of us together at Lake Travis.

A friendly young lady met me at the reception desk. I showed her DJ's picture.

"Sure, I remember that dog," she said.

"He bit one of our volunteers, and unclaimed strays are kept for only seventy-two hours. We put him down on Wednesday. Sorry about that. You should have come for him sooner."

THE MEMORIES OF MY MOTHER'S SUICIDE and the loss of DJ are never far from me, and it seemed with each flight back to Houston, the losses began to weigh heavier on my heart. I returned to Houston in late January to continue working on the video project. On this trip, I wanted to visit a few friends I had known growing up. Each day began with my early morning jog, a quick breakfast at the hotel, and a visit to my parents' gravesite before arriving at the office on time. I had done my best to stay busy to avoid being overwhelmed.

As I drove into the cemetery on Monday morning, I remembered eating tamales with Carol six months earlier in Los Angeles. I reflected on her pointed question to me.

"What are *your* reasons for going to Houston?"

Carol's question had changed everything about these trips.

It was still dark when I arrived at the cemetery. The morning chill made me shiver. When I exhaled, frosted air came from my mouth, and my feet made crunching sounds as I walked across the frozen grass to my parents' graves. At least the cup of coffee I held warmed my hands. The place was empty. It was a perfect chance to take my vengeance and piss on my father's grave. Only the birds in the trees would see.

Yet on this visit, the inner rage I had harbored for so long wasn't there. I tried to conjure it up because anger made me feel strong and superior. To no avail — I couldn't work up the anger like I usually can do. I felt abandoned and alone without it. I finally retreated to sit on the bench and sipped my coffee under the tree as the sky showed the first colored hues of sunrise.

Now singing their morning song, the birds flitted back and forth in the bare branches above my head. Dead in winter, the grass lay thin and yellow-brown under my feet.

Almost like the rising sun, another question surfaced in my mind.

Why do you stay in a prison of anger when the door is unlocked for you?

That question stayed with me for the rest of the week. Each morning I sat on the bench enjoying the sunrise and returned each day after work with fresh flowers for Mom. Andrew and I crossed paths here and there. We made small talk and joked.

"I'll put a shovel in your hands if you keep hanging around here," he joked one afternoon. We laughed like silly boys on the playground.

Andrew never asked me why I came to the cemetery so often. He was obviously a caring sort of man and seemed to understand that I was on a journey.

I often felt like a blind man who was reaching out, feeling his way along.

On Tuesday evening, I met with Denise and her husband. Denise had been a childhood friend I had grown up with at the big church downtown. She was a few years older than me, so I had not known her well as a kid. I remembered her singing solos in church. It was so wonderful men would yell, "Praise the Lord!"

We sat in a quiet corner of the hotel restaurant, talking about childhood memories and old friends. They had read one of my previous books, where I had briefly told my experience of childhood sexual abuse and my addictions as an adult. Denise asked who abused me.

"Gene Lang," I said.

When she heard his name, she slowly leaned back in her chair, nodded, and said, "I thought so."

She then began telling me the long odyssey of *her* childhood nightmare. A relative had sexually abused her. The abuse started when she was five and continued until she was twelve. Then she threw a curveball and told me that she had sexually abused girls younger than her when she was thirteen, and it went on until she was seventeen. As she finished telling her story, her husband began to tell how he was sexually abused as a child. He went on to say that he abused others until he was twenty-two. Finally crushed by guilt and remorse, he turned himself in to the police. He served eight years in prison and will remain a registered sex offender for the rest of his life.

I respect Denise and her husband for not making excuses or trying to explain away their wrongs. I respect how they took responsibility for their actions. Excuses and explanations never change anything. It's what *we do after* we say we're sorry that proves who we are.

THE FOLLOWING DAY I had lunch with a friend named Lee. Lee had been a young pastor at the church on the west side of Houston where my father had played the organ. I was in high school when my father resigned from the downtown church and went to play at the church on the west side. Now in his early seventies, Lee knew me when I dropped out of high school, when I worked on sewage pumps, worked at the rec center, and when I moved to San Diego. Lee had also known my parents for many years.

He was still there on staff when I returned to Houston brokenhearted. Besides my parents, he was the only person in Houston who knew about my drinking. Lee never made me feel like I was a sinner he was trying to get sanctified or a problem he needed to solve. He had a way of seeing good hidden in the shadow of my failures.

I arrived early for our lunch and sat on a bench outside the mom-and-pop Italian restaurant to wait. As they often do, my thoughts drifted back to the night of my mother's suicide.

I thought of how she could have eliminated her pain in a different way. She could have chosen anger and retribution. She could have waited for my father in their room, lying in wait to ambush him. He never would have seen it coming.

Even in the torment of her final moments, she refused herself the hellish satisfaction of vengeance. She gave my father hidden mercy he never thought to see.

Though I didn't know it at the time, I gave my father hidden mercy as well. Something kept me from breaking every bone in his delicate music-playing hands and choking his self-absorbed life out of his blubbery, pale-skinned body. There was protective grace for my father when the police took the gun with them when they left, because I'm not as forgiving as Mom was. I might have shot him myself.

I heard Lee calling to me from across the parking lot. I looked up to see him jogging toward me with his tie flapping in the wind. The hostess seated us at a small table near the back. We sat across from one another. He gave me updates on his wife, his adult children, and their growing bundle of grandchildren, along with new ministries the church was doing in the community. He wanted to know about my life in California, my work in addiction recovery, if I ever still played racquetball, and if I was serious about any woman in my life. *Lee could be a little nosey.*

Halfway through lunch — *I never consciously intended to go there* — I leaned forward and began to quietly tell him — *more like whispering* — what my father said to me the night Mom killed herself. Lee had loved my parents, and by the way his shoulders slumped when I mentioned it, I knew he felt the sadness right along with me.

I was afraid of becoming a blubbering old sot if I looked at him, so I kept my eyes down as I told him the whole story. I told him how my father said he never wanted to marry "that woman" and how furious he was that she wouldn't be there to satisfy his sexual desires. I told him how my father walked out of the room, telling me to clean up the mess in their room. Still looking down, I told of how humiliated I have felt because I did exactly what my father told me to do, like a well-trained servant boy.

I also told Lee I still felt shame for how weak I had been that night and how I wished I had tackled my father to the ground and beat him in the face with my fists.

Sweaty and almost breathless to the point of tears, I finally paused and whispered, "You're the only person I have ever told."

We sat silent for a long minute as I worked to regain my composure.

The waiter refilled our water glasses and slid the check on the table.

Lee quietly broke the silence. "You've never told anyone about this? All these years?"

"No, nobody," I said and shook my head slightly.

"So, you've been alone with this all this time?"

"Yup," I said and nodded.

"You could've hurt him badly that night, but you didn't. In my view, you showed great strength, no matter how it felt to you. You have also guarded him all these years at the expense of your health and happiness. Seems to me you must have loved your father very much."

I shrugged slightly. "Yeah. I guess. I didn't want to humiliate him."

"Wow, David. I respect you for the way you cared for your father. I feel honored you would share this with me, but I must say, when anger and grief go untold for so long, they foster a broken, sad life of deep anguish."

DENISE AND HER HUSBAND put together a small dinner at a steakhouse for the last night I was in town to get me reacquainted with childhood friends I had known from church. I had known some of them since we were four or five years old, sitting on the floor cross-legged in Sunday school. Our teachers read us stories while we placed flannel Bible characters on a flannel-covered board or they used puppet shows to teach us biblical history. Some of these friends were there when I was put out in the hallway for my bad behavior.

At the dinner, there were about fifteen of us. Except for Denise and her husband, I had not seen one of these people in at least forty years.

It had already been a long day for me. I had gone to the cemetery again in the morning and then had a full day of work. I revisited the cemetery in the late afternoon and finally headed to the restaurant. As I was driving to the restaurant, a few questions surfaced in my mind.

Why didn't I run more and eat less these past few weeks?

Why didn't I make time to go back to the hotel to freshen up?

What if these people know about the things I did before I got sober?

As we gathered in a private back room at the steakhouse, I noticed how everyone greeted one another warmly with long hugs. They had never broken the ties of their long friendships. I felt like I had missed out.

Over dinner, we reminisced about summer vacation Bible school, church youth camps, and secrets we kept from our parents. One fellow jokingly mentioned the times I was kicked out to sit in the hallway. I laughed my best laugh so they wouldn't know I still felt embarrassed about it.

Everyone at the dinner had known my father and mother. They mentioned my father with admiration and offered long extravagant condolences for his passing. I nodded with a smile and said, "Thank you."

No one mentioned Mom's suicide, even though the tragic nature of her death was well-known to them all. Word of tragedy spreads fast in churches.

When I realized how utterly exhausted I had become, I was grateful the restaurant was closing. Everyone walked out and we finished our conversations in the parking lot while looking for our keys. I traded phone numbers with some of my old friends. Over the following months, a few of us shared long phone conversations.

Ben, who I remember was one of the smart kids at church, became a chemical engineer with several patents to his credit. Our conversation was often about his twenty-five-year-old son, who struggled with opioid addiction and was in and out of treatment programs. He joyfully told me about his son's artistic talents and the kindness of his heart. Then there were days he cried to me over the phone when his son relapsed.

We spoke of our well-meant, yet futile, efforts to control the behavior of others and how sometimes we are even powerless over ourselves. Our most emotional conversations were about the despair and hopelessness he has experienced since his son died of an overdose.

I knew Jennifer from the junior high group. We lost contact when I went to the new church with my father. She married her high school sweetheart and moved to Nashville, where they raised their family, and she built a career as an agent in the music industry. They divorced thirty years later. She said she had heard of my history with addiction through church gossip, but she never asked questions. We spoke about how she was wounded by marital betrayal and her loneliness with being single again. She told me of her struggle to keep her career afloat and how she was self-destructing with alcohol until she joined a recovery group at her church.

As these conversations grew more honest, our bonds of friendship deepened — I would say even became *intimate*.

Every one of us is wired with the need for intimacy. Our need to tell our stories.

It is our need for *in-to-me-you-see*.

SPRING RENEWAL

THE DAY I WALKED OUT of the dog pound after losing DJ, I was drowning in an ocean of grief, but I didn't know it. Bad decisions are often made when we are confused and alone in our despair. Without knowing exactly what I was setting myself up for, I decided to break a rule that I had made for myself. I got drunk on a weeknight, but that wasn't the end of it.

I got stinking, stammering drunk almost every night for the next three years.

I would stumble home glassy-eyed at two in the morning to pass out on a bed with no sheets. Some nights I puked or peed all over myself while I slept. The next morning, I would spray the mattress with Lysol, flip it over, then drag myself to work while praying, *Please God, don't let it happen again.*

Now and then I sobered up for a week or two. I would run or go to the gym each day and even competed in occasional racquetball tournaments. My father remarried a year after my mother's suicide. I stayed sober the entire week of the wedding celebration to help out.

One night a woman in a bar offered me cocaine. I tried it, and soon I was off and running. Not long after, I discovered heroin and meth. I chased after those twin devils whenever I could. Women came and went. Most were caring and affectionate, but they were too smart to get serious with the drunk and loaded likes of me.

I squandered the money I had saved for a house. I had violent encounters, and several people I knew lost their lives in drug-related violence. My truck was repossessed. Along with it, I lost many of my tools, which I kept in a toolbox bolted behind the cab. I purchased another truck the following week. It was repossessed seven months later, and I lost more of my tools. I bought a third truck, but it was stolen from outside a bar with the rest of my tools.

You cannot work without tools.

Months went by where I didn't pay rent. After being incredibly patient, Graham asked me to move out. To avoid homelessness, I took a job as a handyman and janitor at an apartment complex in return for a studio apartment and forty dollars a week. The tenants were nineteen to twenty-five — students at the University of Texas from well-to-do families. I was twenty-nine, a high school drop-out, a destitute janitor, and a handyman. Most were polite, but they kept their distance as I went about my chores. Others were downright condescending as I fixed their garbage disposals, unplugged their overflowing toilets, and mopped up the messes. There will always be people who want to keep a retard in his place.

I spent my days off sitting in my darkened apartment with the shades drawn, watching television and chain-smoking. I slept twelve to fifteen hours a day. Fridays after work, I walked to the grocery store where I cashed my check, bought canned food, cigarettes, and a twenty-four pack of any beer on sale. I always ran out of food. Then I picked through the dumpster behind the grocery store in the middle of the night. The beer never lasted past Saturday night.

It is hard not to drink when oblivion is your only hope for escape.

I lived there and worked that soul-killing job for fourteen months. It was a long, dark time of waiting, with no immediate end in sight.

One day in the apartment office, I received a message from a good friend, Lauren. She had recently left Austin and returned to her hometown in Southern California, where she met the owner of a swimming pool company in the coastal town of Laguna Niguel. The company needed a repairman, so I called about the job. It turned into an hour-long interview ending with an invitation to interview in person. I borrowed the money for a plane ticket. Two days later, I sat face-to-face with the owner; he hired me on the spot. I gave my notice to the apartment manager, put my possessions in storage, and reported to my new job two weeks later.

When I arrived in Laguna Niguel, all I had was a toolbox, a duffel bag of clothes, and thirty dollars in my pocket. Lauren's brother let me sleep on his couch until I received my first paycheck. Once I got paid, I rented a room within walking distance to work, repaid the money I owed for the plane ticket, and bought a new pair of work boots.

I was the first to work in the morning and usually the last to go home at the end of the day. No request was ever too much. I did side work whenever possible and avoided alcohol and drugs, though I missed them a lot. Within a few months, I had purchased new tools, got my own apartment, had my possessions shipped out, bought a used truck, and had set a little money aside.

I WORKED A YEAR FOR THE COMPANY, then accepted an offer to start a new company with one of my boss's competitors. Our partnership would be fifty-fifty. He would make the sales and I would do the work. A year into it, we both knew our company would never support both of us long-term so I negotiated to buy him out and began building a business of my own.

Within three years, I had a well-trained staff and a thriving business. I'd like to say my skill and smarts made it successful, but I think it was more of my workaholism and compulsive need to please others. Nevertheless, the business afforded me a comfortable home in a quiet neighborhood near the beach. I had nice furniture, new clothes in the closet, and a Corvette in the garage. *A red one, of course.* It was the first home where I finally felt comfortable and safe. It also impressed others.

My need to impress was most apparent in the ways I tried to please my father. I flew back to visit him in Houston as often as I could and stayed in upscale hotels so he would know how much I could afford. I rented upgraded cars, then took him and his new wife to dinner at expensive restaurants. I even bought him a gold watch. One far more expensive than anything I would have ever bought for myself.

I never enjoyed those visits with my father. Time with him was like a reunion with a robot. On the plane home, I always questioned why I had gone. I felt like I owed him for something, but I didn't know what it was. Maybe I was trying to prove that lazy, stupid retards can succeed.

Years into the business, when I was about thirty-four, I began having horrific nightmares several times a month. It was mostly the same dream every time — a violent reflection of my inner world. In my dream, I was walking the streets of Houston in the middle of the night and found myself standing in front of Gene Lang's house. I would pry open a window and silently slink through the house to the bedroom to murder him in his sleep. Or, I would ring his doorbell and hide in the shadows waiting for him to answer the door. Then I would shoot him dead.

I began to drink again on the weekends. Then I started doing drugs again. Weekends began to include Fridays, and then Thursdays, and then Mondays. I began to disappear for a week or more at a time. My staff, business associates, and my neighbors grew terribly concerned. I returned embarrassed and ashamed every time and always promised never to do it again.

There was a woman who stuck around when others didn't. She was an enduring friend. To be discreet, I'll call her Leah. She was a delightfully cute and feisty brunette. She lived in San Diego and worked the afternoon shift at a dingy little bar. Our homes were an hour's drive apart. We visited each other on weekends.

One Saturday when visiting, Leah was vacuuming my living room while I was lying in my recliner watching TV. The noise from the vacuum was irritating me, and I said, "Hey! Do you have to make so much noise? I'm trying to watch TV here."

I was not always the friendliest of hosts.

Leah clicked off the vacuum and glared at me. "You're such an asshole. You need to go to church! If that doesn't straighten you up, nothing will!"

I knew better than to mess with Leah. I wasn't there to see it, but I was told she once punched a guy in the mouth who got handsy with her at work. She hit him so hard a few of his teeth flew out across the dance floor, and everyone applauded!

I liked my teeth, so I wasn't about to argue.

The next morning at nine (like every Sunday she visited after that), we were sitting in the back pew at a local church listening to the preacher. She drank black coffee from Starbucks and fidgeted in her seat. I drank vodka hidden in a Starbucks cup.

One Sunday, the church announced sign-ups for a men's Bible study. Leah elbowed me in the ribs and gave me one of *those* looks. I registered, of course. Several months into the study, I confessed to the men in my group that I had gotten drunk, snorted cocaine, and cheated on Leah the previous weekend. I truly felt horrible about it. The men prayed for me and said, "Be strong in the Lord, brother!"

A month later, I confessed to the same thing. A month after that, another confession. The group taught me that confession is good for the soul as long as you only need to do it once. Confessing to the same thing twice was a problem. Three times was absolutely, without question, unacceptable. The men told me I was a distraction to their Bible study and asked me to leave. One fellow walked me to my truck. He said I was welcome to come back once I was serious about studying the Bible. He also gave me the number for a Christian counselor, who had helped him stop "lusting after women." He was sure that would solve everything.

I went to see that counselor right away. After a dozen appointments, at a hundred and twenty-five bucks a pop, all the counselor kept telling me was that I needed to forgive the sins of others as God had forgiven my sins. This sounded fine and all, except I wasn't feeling very forgiven. Oh…he also told me to get back to church and join a men's accountability group.

How is that for a religious merry-go-round?

A FEW YEARS LATER, I ended up in rehab. It wasn't my idea. It was *the court's* idea. I had been arrested for a small amount of cocaine. The year was 1999; it was a felony back then. Since I had no prior record, I was offered a choice — eighteen months in a treatment program or go to jail. With so much to lose — my business, home, and freedom — I went quickly into treatment, albeit kicking and screaming.

I did not call Leah for a couple of weeks. When I finally did, she said, "I knew something bad happened. You were avoiding me."

Leah had her own backstory. A few years earlier, she had gotten herself in trouble for drugs just like me. She was also a single mom who was working hard to do better than in the past. She wouldn't dare risk the possibility of losing her daughter by being involved with me as I processed through the criminal justice system, and I understood this.

We met for coffee that weekend at a beachside café in Oceanside — about halfway between us — to exchange belongings we had kept at one another's home. She drank coffee and dabbed her eyes with a paper napkin as she cried. I drank decaf — without vodka — and didn't say much.

When it was time to go, I walked her to her car, where we shared a long hug.

"You've filled out a little," she said with a smile while patting my love handles.

Once I quit the drinking and the other stuff, cheeseburgers became irresistible.

I participated in the treatment program Mondays through Fridays from five to nine in the evening and Saturday mornings from nine to eleven. The program included educational lectures twice a week, where I learned about the psychology, biology, and sociology of addiction. This information brought me insight and understanding, which helped soothe my self-hatred. I kept thinking, *Oh my God! Oh my God! Someone knows about this thing inside me. Someone knows!*

I learned that addiction is not a moral failure or a failure of willpower. It is a dysfunction of instinct that hijacks our ability to use our willpower in the best ways. Often induced by trauma, it is malformed thinking, rooted in the same part of the brain that tells us to breathe.

Weekly counseling and drug testing were part of the program. I took part in group therapy sessions five times a week. Right off the bat, I noticed how diverse the others in the group were. It was clear to see how trauma and addiction impact everyone. To hear others tell of the trauma they experienced was a sad but beautiful gift. It was a mercy to discover I was not the only person who ruined their life by how they lived.

The nameplate on my counselor's desk read "Counselor Rob." He had been successful in real estate, with a beachside home in Newport Beach, but had drunk away his fortune. He got sober in his fifties, and now in his late sixties, he loved his work. He was quick with gentle affirmations but even quicker to confront what he saw to be self-sabotaging thinking or behavior. I remember the day he gave me a copy of *The Big Book* from Alcoholics Anonymous.

"What do I do with this?" I asked.

"Read it! What else would you do with it?"

"Hmmm, okay. I've never read a book before."

With a raised eyebrow, he said, "Well, smarty-pants, it's time you get started."

In the past, I had read all kinds of technical manuals for work. I read the newspaper, *Sports Illustrated*, and outdoor magazines like the ones I loved as a boy. As a dedicated church-going teenager, I had also spent lots of time reading the Bible. As I told Counselor Rob, I had honestly never read a book from start to finish.

More than five hundred pages long, *The Big Book* was more than a little intimidating. I started reading small portions at bedtime and quickly learned that reading distracted me from the misery I felt inside. I needed the healthy distraction.

The program also required me to attend 12-step meetings three times a week in addition to the time spent at the treatment center. I was bemoaning this to my neighbor, wondering how I could do it with my schedule. He smiled and said,

"Relax, Dave. There are meetings all the time. I'll take you to one this Sunday night."

"You can't!" I said. "You have to be an alcoholic to go."

"Ever see me drink? I've been going to meetings for seven years."

"What?! Why didn't you ever tell me?"

With a shrug, he said, "There's a reason it's called 'anonymous.'"

The meeting was in a local community center ten minutes from my house. It was packed with more people than you could count. While my neighbor went in, I stopped outside to join a dozen others for a smoke — my last smoke before the firing squad. Once inside, I noticed again how people had come from all walks of life. Some were heavily tattooed and wildly pierced. Others were immaculately dressed in designer clothes and with perfectly styled hair.

My neighbor found our seats near the back. I slouched as low in mine as a grown man could possibly slouch. Once the meeting started, people stood up to talk (or *share* as I came to learn). There was something familiar and repulsive about each one of them. They were like a bunch of retards, except they seemed pretty happy with themselves and to be with other retards.

I then heard a familiar voice start speaking. It was someone I knew from the gym. When I looked around the room, I saw a clerk from the grocery store, an attendant at the local gas station, and a man I had built a swimming pool for. I slouched even lower and began to weep. I did not want to be a retard again, and I slouched lower still.

I was sniffling and went to wipe my nose with my sleeve. A small hand reached back from the seat in front of me and handed me a small packet of tissues. The hand belonged to a young woman with tattoos on her arms and neck. She peered back at me over her shoulder. Her eyes were bright and clear, and her eyeliner was thick as road tar. She whispered, "Go ahead, take it. It's what we do for one another around here."

I LOOKED FORWARD to the sessions with Counselor Rob. He was intuitive, gentle, and interested to know how I came to be who I was. He was also direct and could be grumpy at times. He made sure that I had an experienced sponsor from the 12-step meetings.

Counselor Rob and my sponsor understood that when I was *working the steps* honestly, the steps were also working me. As a result, my addictions became truth-telling prophets that spoke from the grave of my self-destructiveness. I began to understand how my *head* was blind to see the hurt my heart had known. New courage emerged, a willingness to confront the lies I believed about myself.

Thursday night was Family Night at the center. It was a time for clients to bring spouses, or perhaps parents, and sometimes even adult children to participate in a community discussion. There were usually about fifty of us. We sat in a large circle. Leah was not going to be there, and I did not have anyone else, so I went to Family Night alone.

Several months into the program, my father was in Southern California for a music conference. He accepted my invitation to attend Family Night. We sat side by side in the circle. Counselor Rob was the facilitator. When it was my father's turn to speak, he spoke as if he was the smartest person in the room.

"I'm glad to see David is here to get help. He has always had problems following the rules and staying out of trouble. It's been exhausting to his mother, God rest her soul, and to me. Keep up the good work. I pray he learns his lesson this time."

At our next session, Counselor Rob asked me about Family Night with my father.

"How was your time with your father?"

"It was fine."

"What did you two talk about while he was here?"

"Not much. We had dinner, then we went to Family Night. He had things to do the next day before he flew home."

"That was it? You didn't talk about Family Night?"

"Nope."

"Did anything at Family Night bother you?"

"Nope. Not that I recall. It was all good."

Counselor Rob saw what I couldn't. I was blind to notice the knife-edged slashing of my father's humiliating words in public. Years of absorbing his contempt had so groomed me that even as an adult, I was willing to bear his public scorn without a thought of defending myself.

Counselor Rob assigned me homework every week, and he was a stickler for it to be finished on time. After Family Night, he gave me a different kind of assignment.

"Here's a few short questions you should answer for yourself."

What keeps me from appreciating myself?
Why do I work so hard, as if I'll never have enough?
What am I trying to prove?
Why am I afraid of success?

That *short assignment* took me a month to complete. Each week Counselor Rob asked me about it, but he gave me extra time to finish. Once I had finally worked the questions through, I talked them over with him *and* my sponsor. The process of answering the questions began to peel away the subconscious blindness I had used to protect myself since I was a boy.

I had to face the scars inflicted by my father.

I had to face the music.

SIX MONTHS INTO THE PROGRAM, Counselor Rob had another question to ask me.

"You claim to be a Christian, right?"

"Yes, sir!" I proudly replied. "Born and raised; church three times a week since I was a kid."

"That is wonderful! Tell me about Jesus. Tell me all about God."

His question was no surprise to me. Counselor Rob was happy to tell you he was a man of faith. He called himself a "recovering Catholic" and at the same time spoke of going to Mass twice a week and loving it. On his shelves, next to the books about addiction and psychotherapy, and 12-step texts, were a couple of Bibles and other books from all kinds of religious writers.

I did not hold back in my response. Right from the get-go, I let him know we were all born sinners. Then, with a surprising amount of recall, I told Counselor Rob of the preacher's authoritative messages. I described what I learned from the flannelgraph images and puppet shows in Sunday School. I detailed the looks on people's faces that I saw run down the aisles to get their souls signed, sealed, and delivered for Jesus.

Counselor Rob listened with interest as I waxed eloquently with my religious expertise. After a few minutes, he raised his hand and said in an exasperated voice, "Stop! That is enough! I don't want to hear one more word of that malarkey!"

As you can imagine, I was offended and gave him my best evil-eye stare. It didn't have much impact. Counselor Rob didn't even blink but went on to say, "I'm not buying what you think you're selling, and I don't think you buy it either."

Now I was really steamed, but he wasn't finished.

"Look at your life. No matter what you say or how you try to spin it, you are functionally an atheist. I think you better find a real Jesus. I think you need to find a real God."

I wanted to storm out of his office, slamming the door behind me. Quite frankly, I'm surprised I didn't. I just said, "How can you say that?"

Counselor Rob softened his tone. "Well, ask yourself, whatever you claim to believe, why isn't it working for you?"

I was dumbfounded.

Later that evening, I met my sponsor at a late-night coffee shop. It was a cold, damp evening, yet I waited for him outside so I could smoke. Standing there puffing my lungs out, I was haunted by the question, "Why isn't it working?"

I was deep in debt. I had lost my girlfriend. My father hardly wanted to speak to me unless it was to humiliate me. Many friends were keeping their distance. Business associates were sticking around only for their financial benefit. I had overdosed several times. I was in a long-term rehab program that was stretching me beyond my limits. The worst part of it all was that I still craved alcohol and drugs more than anything.

For the first time I saw how powerless I was to stop destroying myself. I was emptier than empty inside and admitted to myself that my religious professions had left me morally and spiritually bankrupt. Desperate, and not knowing what else to do, I looked up at the stars and said, "Oh God! I am a drug addict. I am absolutely clueless about who you are. I will call you any name you want me to, but if you don't help me, I'm afraid I'm going to die."

Perhaps you've heard the term *moment of clarity*?

In that moment, a small nugget of personal honesty was unearthed inside me. I accepted myself for who I was — a man in dire need. Everything suddenly seemed unimportant except one thing — God. Either God would help me, or I was a walking dead man.

As I stood there alone with nothing but my pathetic prayer and a half-empty pack of Marlboros, I heard a voice say, "Alright, David, now I can go to work."

I whirled around to see who had spoken but saw no one there. I thought maybe my sponsor had shown up and was hiding, playing a joke on me. I looked behind the bushes next to the coffee shop. No one was there either. Then I looked around the cars in the parking lot. Again, no one was there. I finally ran over to look behind the dumpster twenty yards away. *Nobody.*

Maybe I was going crazy, I thought. Yet I also sensed that maybe something good had arrived. Whatever or whoever it was, I knew my prayer had been heard, and when it responded, it called me by name. I knew my battles had been joined by something powerful enough to change what needed changing. *Me!*

When my sponsor finally arrived, I told him what happened. We talked about it for hours. It was well after midnight when I arrived home. As I crawled into bed, I wasn't sure if it was a spiritual experience or if I had fallen into the abyss of insanity. In the shower the following morning, as the water poured over me, I asked myself, *Did that really happen?*

The Voice spoke again.

"I am here. Yesterday was a good day. Let's go do it again, together."

At the treatment center that afternoon, I briefly spoke with Counselor Rob in the hallway and told him of my late-night experience. He smiled and said, "I doubt you're going crazy. In fact, you look better than I've ever seen you look. I bet you and your friend working together can build a life worth living. Now get to bed on time!"

I continued to hear the Voice and responded to it like I would to a trusted friend. It became an ongoing dialogue. The Voice was gentle and powerful, always in solidarity with my soul, a deep current of identification and understanding. I started to secretly call it, *My Friend the Voice*, but I wasn't about to tell many people. They would think I had gone looney tunes.

OVER THE NEXT FEW MONTHS, I grew more and more curious.

I kept wondering to myself, *Who is 'My Friend the Voice'?*

I began to investigate by reading. I read a Buddhist book which I found helpful, but it didn't explain *My Friend the Voice*. I read self-help books and psychology books, which were also useful. I even read a book that promised cosmic power from crystals and gemstones. I don't have much to say about that one. I thought of reading the Bible but I told myself, "No way!"

That was the craziest idea yet.

While driving home from the treatment center late on a Saturday morning, I thought about *My Friend the Voice*. It had been months since our first encounter. I thought about the Bible again. I still had one that Mom had given me years before. I pulled it out of a box buried in the garage when I got home.

When I sat down to read, I was blindsided by a psycho-wacky roadblock. (That's the best clinical way I can describe it.) When I saw the word "God" on the page — G-O-D — rage flashed red inside me. I stood up and walked out of the room. A while later, after a smoke, I returned to try again.

This time I read the word J-E-S-U-S. Just seeing the letters made me throw the Bible across the room.

Now here's something interesting. In all the reading I had been doing, I had seen the words *God* and *Jesus* more times than I could count. Visceral anger came over me when I saw them on the pages of Scripture. I kept trying to read on and off throughout the afternoon, but it always ended the same way. *Rage!*

That night in bed, as I was reading AA's *Big Book*, I internally said to *My Friend the Voice, If you want me to read the dang Bible, you're going have to help me. If not, I'll find something else to read.*

Just before I turned off the lights, the Voice whispered back, *If you can't stand to see G-o-d on the page, put your finger over it and replace it in your mind with the word "Truth." And if you can't handle the letters J-e-s-u-s, put your finger over them and replace them with the word "Love."*

The following Sunday morning, I came home after an AA meeting and breakfast with friends, and gave the "finger over the word" exercise a try. It was cumbersome, but it moved me beyond the hijacking power of anger. A dozen chapters into it, I didn't need to cover G-o-d or J-e-s-u-s every time I saw those words. In a few days, this is how the Story began to unfold for me.

For Truth so loved the world that Truth gave Love, and anyone who trusts in the Love that Truth gives isn't going to die.

In the sermons I heard growing up, troubled people in the Bible often seemed to be minimized as stage props to explain theology and the ever-important role of the church. As I read, I was struck by the way Jesus related with weak, brokenhearted people. He placed them on the main stage, front and center in his attention.

In the Gospels of Matthew and Mark, I read about a woman who had been chronically ill for twelve years. Her life was ruined. She hid in the gathered crowd in the story, hoping to be healed by touching Jesus' clothes. When she had the chance, she secretly reached out to grab the healing she needed.

The story says that with her touch, Jesus felt power leave him. I can just see Jesus whirling around, saying, "Hey! Who just pickpocketed my power?!"

If that had happened to me, I would have chased down that sneaky power-grabbing thief and gotten my power back because I know I'd need it. However that is not what Jesus did. He calmly turned and asked who it was. He knew that he had power to spare.

The next part is the best. The woman could have ignored Jesus to avoid embarrassment. She could have played it safe and pretended she wasn't the one who did such a silly, desperate thing — but she didn't! She didn't run or hide or play it safe! She mustered the courage to respond to him in front of everyone. She let everyone see who she was.

Perhaps the most ignored part of this story is that Jesus never asked her *why* she had done such a thing. His only response was, "Take heart; your faith has healed you."

This powerful story gave me the courage to listen for the call of healing and to go after it just like that weak yet bold woman had done.

Later in the Gospel of Mark, I read about a father whose son had a life-threatening condition. Again, with courage born out of desperation, he stepped out of the crowd to ask Jesus *if he was willing* to help his son. In front of everyone, Jesus pushed back against the man. "What do you mean 'if'? The question isn't *if* I am willing. Of course, I'm willing. The true question is whether or not you believe it's possible."

In an amazing expression of desperate hope, one that retards and addicts and the painfully infirmed will understand, the man said, "Yes, I believe! I believe! Now please help me in my unbelief!"

As I read this man's words, I was struck with a deep, abiding respect for him. He was willing to do whatever he had to do to get help for his son, even risk exposure and ridicule for his fear and weak faith. In the end, Jesus healed the man's son. God's response to weak faith is miracle-making power.

Later on, I read about a blind beggar sitting at his usual place, collecting his daily scraps, when he heard the commotion of a crowd following Jesus. He started yelling, "Notice me! Notice me! Help me! Help me! Have mercy on me!" (At least, this is my way of telling it.)

Everyone told the blind man to shut up and be quiet, but he yelled all the louder. His cries were so loud they got Jesus' attention. Jesus called for the blind man to be brought to him. He jumped up and went straight to Jesus as fast as he could.

"What do you want from me?" asked Jesus.

The blind man's simple response? "I want to see."

Think about this for a minute. For his whole life, blindness was all the man knew. No doubt he had learned to live with it, but he deeply wanted more. He lived with the constant pain of not knowing what others could see. He knew he was powerless to see and really know what he was missing. After such a life, it makes sense that his only desire would be the simple gift of sight.

Just as he had with the ill woman, Jesus affirmed the blind man's faith as essential to his healing. It was at that moment, standing with Jesus, the blind man discovered he could see.

As I read this story, the beggar inside of me noticed this man was far more than just a blind beggar. I saw his strength and dignity. I knew the desperation that gave him the courage to cry out for help. The big takeaway came in the form of two questions.

What is it that I am blind to see?

How desperate am I?

I didn't know the answers because I was clueless (and still am in many ways) about what I could not see. Yet, the desperate hope of the blind beggar had illuminated the way of faith. The awareness of my blindness and my desperate desire to see were the beginning of my healing.

After reading the gospels, I moved on to the book of Acts and read about the daily followers of Jesus. Oh my goodness! Don't even get me started about those well-intentioned but ego-fueled whack-a-doodles. It seems that most of them — how should I say it? — didn't play very well with others. No matter what I say, we can't ignore the depth of their passion. Given the social prejudices they faced as Jesus followers, it is miraculous they kept true to their journey. They were amongst something — *Someone* — bigger than themselves.

Out of all of Jesus' followers, I think Paul is the most *interesting* one of all. If you want to righteously compare yourself to anyone, stand next to him. Before he became a Jesus follower, he was a murderer. He even admitted it, never hiding his evil history. He actually called himself "the worst of all sinners." *Whew!* Sigh of relief! I already felt better.

After Acts, I continued to the book of Romans, which incidentally was written by that ex-murderer, Paul. I arrived at the middle of the seventh chapter where he states — this is my paraphrase — "I want to do good, but I don't. I don't want to do wrong, but I end up doing it anyway. It seems that something is terribly wrong inside of me. For I know what is right, but I can't always trust myself to do the right thing. I'm a man who's in trouble way over his head. Who will help and rescue me?"

I could not have said it any better. I kept thinking, *Oh my God! It sounds like Paul struggles with addiction like me!*

When I turned the page and came to the eighth chapter,

Paul says in essence, "I can only thank you, God. No one who knows Jesus Christ will be condemned."

When I read that, I sat back in my chair and took a long, deep breath. I held it a long time before I let it go. With that breath came a realization.

I said out loud to myself…

My Friend the Voice speaks from the heart of Jesus.

A SAYING I HEARD IN RECOVERY meetings was, "God will do for us what we can't do for ourselves." There is a flip side to this that makes a lot of sense to me.

God won't do for us what only we can do for ourselves.

I discovered these two truths as I stumbled, bumbled, and face-planted myself into being an accidental but intentional follower of Jesus.

Looking at the memory of the parking lot where I first heard *My Friend the Voice*, I realized I never had an honest connection with God until that anguished moment when I asked for it. I believe my desperate plea for salvation was evidence that something much bigger was already at work inside me. Perhaps there was something incredible inside all of us that wouldn't become fully alive until we were desperate enough to ask for it. Maybe we had to leave the God we were told to believe in so we could find the God who is intimately revealed inside of us?

One year into the treatment program, I received a chip that marked one year of sobriety. I never imagined staying sober for that long. It felt good to hold it in my hand. On the one hand, I always knew what I was doing was wrong, but on the other, I felt miserable without alcohol and drugs.

Not to worry though, after a year, things settled down for me emotionally. I remember thinking, *This recovery thing isn't too bad. Maybe I'll keep doing this for a while and see what happens. I can always go back if I need to.*

When I completed the program six months later. I was totally out of debt and felt emotionally healthier than I had ever felt. I turned my attention back to my business, making it simpler and more efficient. I made improvements to my home. I also kept going to the 12-step meetings because I knew I had failed so many times before and I used my past failures to motivate me.

Fear of relapse is a good thing.

I also went back to that church Leah had dragged me to.

Others who were new in the recovery meetings began to ask me for help, which I was glad to give because my sponsor and others had given so much to me. I was grateful for every one of them. They thought I was helping them, and I guess I was. They had no idea how much they were helping me. I was still concerned for my long-term growth, so I decided to go to psychotherapy. I thought it would help me quit smoking and stop using bad language.

A few months into therapy, I started having angry outbursts when we discussed the trips I had made to see my father. I also had an upcoming trip to see him in a couple months. Week after week, my therapist and I spoke about this trip until I finally yelled out, "I don't want to go. I-just-do-not-want-to-*effing*-go!"

My therapist replied with the syrupy-sweet calmness he often used, which irritated me to no end. "Then ask yourself a question. *Why are you going?*"

Another question that got my heart's attention.

I spent the next three nights crafting a short letter to my father. My letter said that I had come to understand the hurtful way he treated my mother, sister, and me. If he wanted to have a relationship with me, he would have to face how his anger and use of pornography had hurt us as a family. I also said that if he was not willing, I would break off contact until he was. I closed the letter by offering to fly to Houston weekly to attend family therapy as father and son.

I wanted to be direct but respectful, so I asked my 12-step sponsor and therapist to look over the letter. They approved of its tone and content. That night I called my father to let him know I was emailing the letter, but I didn't tell him what it said. His response was, "Okay, sure. I've got people from church over. I'll read it tomorrow and call you back."

That one-minute phone call was the last time my father ever spoke to me.

The year was 2001.

For the next four years I hurried home every day after work to check my email. I was like a little boy running home after school as fast as he could go, hoping to find his father there to meet him as promised. My father never was there. The response I needed from him never came. There was only that same emptiness I had always known from him.

I was complaining to my sponsor about my father's silence. He looked at me and said, "It seems that you've already got your answer. The question is, 'Will you face it and move on?'"

Yet still, I held out hope. It took me all four of those years, and then some, to let go of the fantasy that my father might come through for me. My father's final silence brought my hurt, and my anger, to a full boil.

About the same time, I still attended the church Leah had dragged me to. They asked me to start a group to help men addicted to porn. My response was emphatic: "No!"

Regardless of what I said, those darn church folk wouldn't let me off the hook. A few months later, two men and I sat down and began applying the 12-steps to the most sensitive areas of our lives. Within a year, there were more than thirty men in the room. We listened to one another as each of us spoke of our weakness and shame. We were limping, lurching examples of imperfect honesty, stumbling and bumbling our way forward, imparting hope to one another along the way. It was hard work, and our most divine glory. The only price we had to pay was our ego.

After the meetings, I stayed up late into the night, writing down everything I could remember from our conversations. Those notes became my first book, *When Lost Men Come Home — Not for Men Only*.

The little fisherman diagnosed as "mentally retarded" had become an author.

My pool company survived my addictions, but the recession of 2009 sunk it. I sold the Corvette, my motorcycles, and my unused construction equipment. Last to go, I put up my home for sale. With little to do with my free time, I followed a suggestion from a friend and went to school to become an addiction counselor. It was a five-year program, but I got it done in two, made straight As, and I went to work in the addiction treatment field.

Even us retards can go back to school and do good.

I always enjoyed working with clients and patients. However, within a few years, I saw that my best work was in writing and speaking. This is what led me to work with the video production team in Houston.

To my astonishment, not giving up on myself was the road that led me home.

BETWEEN TRIPS TO HOUSTON to work on the videos, I took a vacation. At four o'clock on a Thursday morning, I fired up my motorcycle and began the long trek from my home in California to meet friends in Estes Park, Colorado. They were coming from Omaha, Nebraska. Our plan was to spend a week together riding motorcycles and camping.

Heading east from where I live, there is no way to avoid the Mojave Desert. It's a gargantuan landscape of immense beauty and danger. It was late spring, so by eight in the morning, the wind was hot enough to suck the water out of me before my armpits could even think about sweating. The best time to get through the Mojave is in the early morning before sunrise.

Bats and birds flashed in and out of my headlight. They flew just above the ground, looking for a morsel. Rattlesnakes were out on the road to soak up the heat from the asphalt. There were lots of rabbits. They scampered back and forth as if playing chicken with the wheels of my motorcycle. I felt *thump-thump* when they got it wrong. They became instant fast food for the birds and desert varmints.

As the sun rose, cacti appeared out of the dark like prickly ghosts — guardians of a dangerous land. Long hours in the saddle across the Mojave gave me plenty of time to think. I tried to abide in God's presence as I ventured into this difficult stretch of road, but I wasn't very good at it. Apprehension lingered close. It reminded me how pathetic my faith could be. This was one reason why I was grateful for the gentle way God showed up for me. The history and dogma of my toxic religious upbringing had given me no strength until *My Friend the Voice* met me in my most painful time of need.

As I rode toward the morning sunrise, I thought again about the night Mom shot herself. I don't think there has been a day since it happened that I've not thought of it. It was so obvious that Mom loved my father more than she loved herself. No doubt this was a core element to her sickness. I remembered facing my father in that bloody room. I took a moment and thanked God that I didn't react with violence that night.

To recenter my heart in gratitude, I challenged myself with questions.

What would have happened had I killed my father?

How many years would I have been locked away?

As I pondered these questions, I heard *My Friend the Voice* whisper over the sound of the rushing wind.

Build your future by looking for the hidden mercy. Even on the night your mom killed herself. Think of the mercy she had for your father — and the protective mercy God had for you.

As I rolled into my first stop for the night west of Flagstaff, I thought about meeting my friends in Estes Park. It would be five other men and me. Three were senior staff at a Christian church in Omaha. The others were influential benefactors. In years prior, the church had hired me several times to come speak to their community about addiction and inspire spiritual growth for recovery.

I remembered how nervous I felt the first time I spoke there. The church's senior leader, Dr. Kris, had been a student of my father at the university in Houston fifty years before. He was in his twenties at the time. He was also a junior staffer at the first church where my father played the organ, and had known Gene Lang, as everyone at the church did. Dr. Kris knew my father as a respected professor — a revered church musician — and me as a misbehaving child. More than once, he had been asked to escort me out of classes or activities where I was being a problem.

Decades later, Dr. Kris learned of my work in addiction recovery. We have become dear friends over the years. Outside our professional responsibilities, he is just Kris to me.

The shame of Houston haunted me when I accepted Kris's offer that first time to speak. Despite my hesitation, I went to do the work anyway. To my surprise, it became an experience of great healing. Kris was also the one who invited me on this motorcycle trip. Joining us on the ride was Ted, a long-time colleague of Kris. Ted was also from Houston and had known my father.

After a good night's sleep, I was back on the road in the morning before sunrise. As I neared Flagstaff, the air temperature dropped to near freezing. I saw elk crossing the road twice, so I slowed in case one darted out in front of me. To make things even more challenging, the rising sun was blinding me in the eyes. With the harsh sunlight, the cold, and the need to be hyper-alert, I was exhausted by breakfast time. Nevertheless, with five hundred miles to cover that day, I rode straight through Flagstaff and kept going. The temperature rose to over a hundred as I rode past the Four Corners area of Arizona, New Mexico, Utah, and Colorado. I turned north on the first paved road toward the mountains in search of cooler temperatures. I passed through Cortez, then Durango, and finally pulled over for the night near Pagosa Springs. I pitched my tent beside a twisty, gurgling mountain stream and took a freezing bath in the crisp water before crawling into my sleeping bag for the night.

I HEADED NORTH THE NEXT MORNING over Wolf Creek Pass into the heartland of Colorado. The roads twisted through glorious green alpine passes, past sweet-smelling fields and farmhouses that looked like pictures on a postcard. I stopped to rest in the towns of Creede and Gunnison, then rode over Wilkerson Pass and up to the top of Pike's Peak. I stopped in Woodland Park to stay for the night with my friends, Melany and Les. For twenty-five years, they've run a youth camp that sits at the foot of Pike's Peak. Les wrangles the horses, the wildlife, and the wild-natured boys. Melany, a master chef, feeds everyone like royalty and wrangles Les, because somebody has to.

After saying goodbye the next morning, I continued on my way. I saw small herds of elk, deer, a few bighorn sheep, and mountain goats on the higher passes. Although it is a challenge, I prefer to travel on two wheels. I feel too insulated inside of a car. When I'm on a motorcycle, I feel and smell the air. I have a sense of connection with everything around me. Yes, there are risks, and I have had mishaps. I know I am exposed and vulnerable. This is when I feel the most alive.

I arrived in Estes Park on the third day, where Kris, Ted, and the others greeted me with smiles and hugs. After wolfing down lunch and filling our tanks, we headed west out of town. The road took us up endless twists and turns as we snaked ever higher into the treeless thin-air passes of Trail Ridge Road, and then back down into the high-country forest. We turned off and pitched our tents in a field for the night near Lake Granby.

After setting up our campsite, we gathered around a campfire to chat during the fading daylight. I sat down next to Kris, looking for a conversation about the Houston we had known decades ago. Kris knew that my father and I had not spoken for years. He was kind enough not to ask why. While the rest of the guys talked about the day's ride, Kris and I talked about our memories of Houston and the people we knew there. He smiled as he told me about being my father's student and how my father was admired as a teacher and musician. I could tell he really liked my father. I bristled inside a little, but I didn't interrupt.

Out of the blue, Kris said, "Oh! I remember your father had those tiger's-eye cufflinks. They were amazing. I had never seen anything like it, before or since."

Until Kris mentioned it, I had forgotten about my father's tiger's-eye jewelry.

My father often bought raw, unfinished tiger's-eye gemstones. He would pay a local gemologist to polish them in a tumbler. It took weeks for them to be finished. When they finally came back, the stones glistened with colors of brown, bronze, and gold, as if they glowed from the inside. My father then had them mounted as cufflinks, tie clasps, or bracelets.

I remember people at church oohing and aahing over his tiger's-eyes. Those rocks made him shine with popularity. On my seventh birthday, I was thrilled when my father pinned one of his tiger's-eye tie clasps on my tiny little tie as we headed out the front door to church. *We were tiger's-eye twins for the day.*

After we broke camp the next morning, my friends and I spent the next two days exploring the back roads of Colorado as we meandered west toward Moab, Utah. Once we were there, we settled into a hotel for much-needed air conditioning and to get some laundry done. We all smelled pretty gamey at that point!

The plan for the next day was to explore some of the dirt roads around Arches National Park, but Ted's bike wasn't set up for dirt roads. He chose to hang out in Moab, and I chose to stay with him. After the others took off, Ted and I had breakfast, then we strolled from one side of town to the other. We came to a curio shop at the north end of town.

"Let's check it out," Ted said. "I want to get something for my sons."

The store inside was a mesmerizing collection of native artifacts, dinosaur fossils, precious stones, handmade Western knives, and silver jewelry made with turquoise, topaz, and tiger's-eye. The jewelry was encased under lights in glass displays. While Ted looked for gifts for his sons, I went back outside and ambled my way down a long row of rusty metal bins. The bins were filled with petrified wood, small, broken dinosaur bones and fossils, loose mineral stones, clumps of unrecognizable crystals, and piles of unfinished gemstones. At the end of the row, the last bin was half filled with rocks covered in mud and silt. They looked like the dirt clods my buddies and I used to throw at each other in our dirt-clod fights. Above the bin hung a wood sign with faded lettering. *Raw tiger's-eye - $2 each.*

I stopped in my tracks and stared at the sign. It seemed to stare back, challenging me to a fight. My thoughts went back to the campfire conversation with Kris and the memory of my father pinning his tiger's-eye tie clasp on me. As I stared at the sign, I heard *My Friend the Voice.*

You have two dollars. That's more than enough for what you need.

Just then, Ted walked up with his purchases in a brown paper bag and asked, "Whatcha looking at?" He looked and saw the sign above the bin, then said, "Hey, I remember your dad wore those tiger's-eye cufflinks to church all the time. Man, they were something!"

With that, he turned and nonchalantly walked the other way.

Once he turned his back, I reached into the bin and pulled out a medium-sized stone. As I walked to the front door to pay for it, some of the crusted dirt on the tiger's-eye began to fall away. I could see a hint of beauty in it.

The clerk at the counter glanced at it. "Just one tiger's-eye? That's all you want? Two dollars, please."

I walked back outside and began rubbing the stone in my hands to remove more of the silt. Then I put it in the left front pocket of my motorcycle pants. I closed the zipper on the pocket and folded the Velcro flap over the top to be doubly sure I wouldn't lose it.

When our group reassembled, we rode south and then west through the Capitol Reef area, then camped near the small town of Torrey. The next morning, we rode down the Escalante Staircase, a narrow, twisty, tar-snaked road that runs along the top of a ridgeline for miles, with dangerous cliffs on both sides. Every few miles, I dropped my left hand off the handlebar to feel the tiger's-eye in my pocket. I was afraid to lose it.

On our last day, we got hotel rooms near Bryce Canyon and spent the evening sitting in a circle outside our rooms, telling stupid jokes while eating pizza and ice cream. My friends headed north the following day to ride through Idaho and Wyoming on their way back to Omaha. I headed south to visit the North Rim of the Grand Canyon, then back through Flagstaff and the Mojave for home.

On the long stretches of the interstate, I rested my hand on my thigh to feel the tiger's-eye in my pocket. I thought of when I was a boy and needed affirmation from my father. I was a terribly sad child for not getting it. I thought of the poignant saying: *The hardest apology to accept is the one never given.*

I asked myself, "How much sadness have I suffered from wallowing in the fantasy of wishing things were different from what they are?"

I spent the night in Kingman, Arizona. The next morning, I was on the road at four to avoid the worst of the desert heat on my last leg home. With the sun rising behind me, and my hand resting on the lump of stone in my pocket, I thought of how hard it is for me to surrender anger when I think it is righteous. I considered stopping, getting off my bike, and hurling the stone into the desert where it would never be found.

From a place deep inside, where *My Friend the Voice* and I meet, I spoke these words out loud.

My father never apologized because he just couldn't bring himself to do such a thing.

I don't need to know the reasons why.

ONCE I WAS BACK HOME, I couldn't find the tiger's-eye. I cussed at myself for three days for losing it until it reappeared in the bottom of the washing machine — the unofficial lost and found department at my house. The agitation of the soapy water had washed off all the remaining dirt and smoothed the edges a little, which revealed more of the hidden colors. It clearly looked like one of the stones my father loved so much. I felt joyously relieved when I found it. The sense of loss, but then finding it again, showed how much I valued it. I placed it in a sandwich baggie for safekeeping and hung it on the wall next to the picture of Andrew and me. It was the symbol of a journey. Not my father's journey, but my journey.

Several weeks later, I tossed the sandwich baggie with the tiger's-eye into my briefcase and left for the airport to go to Houston. It was my final assignment to finish the last of my work. It was a Sunday afternoon; rain was pouring down as the plane took off. When I landed in Houston, the weather was unseasonably cool for June, and the air felt desert dry.

As usual, I began Monday with an early morning jog, ate breakfast at the hotel, picked up flowers for Mom, and headed to the cemetery with the tiger's-eye in my pocket. As expected, the cemetery was almost empty. The sun was already bright as it rose in the eastern sky. The birds sang and flitted in the trees. The groundskeepers were beginning their work.

I walked straight from my rental car to my parents' graves and set the flowers down on the grass next to my mother's side of their headstone.

Hello, Mom. Love you.

I pulled the stone from my pocket and paused to think for a moment. I thought of the years I had been emotionally subservient to my father and how much sanity it had cost me. I thought again of pissing on his grave, but that felt unnecessary now. I also thought of chucking the tiger's-eye across the cemetery as far as I could throw it. This tiger's-eye, however, was not only for my father. It was also for me.

For reasons I'm not sure of, maybe as a reminder lest I forget this moment of surrender years down the road, I used my phone to take a picture of the tiger's-eye. I held it steady in my hand.

Click!

With the sound of the click, I thought of my mom and how she treasured moments with her loved ones. I took a second to email the picture to myself so I would never lose the moment.

In contrast to the anger I felt when I had first brought flowers from the Indian woman and her cranky husband, I felt no striking emotion as I placed the tiger's-eye on the headstone next to my father's name. *Here you go, Dad. This is for you.*

Then I calmly sat down on *my bench* under the tree for a few minutes before leaving for work.

As it turned out, the workload was light that week. I used the extra time to visit many of the memorable childhood places I had visited in the past year. I drove to the house on Sandpiper Street. When I pulled up, I thought of the stormy day when Mrs. Davidson saw me make-believe fishing and sent Mr. Davidson to guide me safely home. I looked at their front lawn where I played football with Daniel and the older boys. It was tiny compared to what I remembered. I wished the Davidsons could see how strong I had grown up to be.

I drove to the sports park and found an unlocked gate to one of the baseball fields. I walked around the bases and imagined running them as a boy.

The following day I drove to see the little old white house on Glenlea Street. This time, I got out and stood for a few minutes in front of my old home. Then I slowly strolled up the street and stopped in front of Mr. and Mrs. Hargis' house. Then I walked to the end of the block, crossed the street, and took my time walking down the other side. A man in his driveway washing his eighties-something Oldsmobile gave me a soapy-handed wave and said, "Good morning!"

"Good morning to you, sir. Great car," I replied and waved back.

"I can't believe the weather," he said while making long swirls with his sponge. "It's too nice outside not to enjoy it. You have a good one!"

"Yes, sir. Same to you."

A few houses further, an elderly woman was watering plants on her front porch. It was the house where Sofia and her family had lived. She looked at me curiously with squinted eyes of suspicion while adjusting her glasses. She set down her watering bucket and hobbled across her lawn to the sidewalk. "Hey there, young man. You ain't from around here. You lost, honey?"

"No, ma'am. I'm not lost, but thank you."

"I know you ain't from around here. You lookin' for somethin'? You in trouble?" she asked again.

"No, ma'am. Truth is, I lived here a long time ago. It's taken me a while to find my way back."

"Well, glory be, goodness' sakes. Must be quite a story behind that," she said, shaking her head a bit. She stared at me for a moment longer, her suspicion seemed to subside, and she went back to her watering.

I walked around the entire block, then returned to my rental car and slowly drove away.

EVERY MORNING THAT WEEK, like every other week in Houston, I went to the cemetery with fresh flowers for Mom, then sat on my bench under the tree.

On my last afternoon in Houston, I went to the cemetery to say goodbye to my parents. I had no idea when I would return. I hadn't seen Andrew all week, so I asked one of the groundskeepers, who told me he was on vacation. I imagined him lounging with his wife on a beach in Maui, drinking colorful libations with those little paper umbrellas. Or perhaps he was sitting in a boat with his son on a lake, teaching him how to fish. Wherever he was, I was glad for him.

I took my place under the tree and watched the grounds crew collect the dead, faded flowers. I had seen this before; it was the reason I brought fresh flowers for Mom each time. I also noticed the crew had left the tiger's-eye on the headstone for the entire week. They had seen me sitting there many times and I took it as a personal kindness.

A question came to me as I sat there.

Was my father buried wearing his tiger's-eye cufflinks?

There was no way for me to know. No one informed me of my father's death or his funeral until my cousin Brian called days after it was all over.

Yet with that question, I remembered how he had made sure Mom was buried wearing her opal mosaic, and I felt a measure of gratitude for him. Then it dawned on me how far I had come to bury my father with a tiger's-eye, and I felt thankful for the journey that led me here.

I thought of how my parents were still alive inside of me — for good and for bad. Nothing would ever change that, and I felt pleased with it. I remembered all the trips to Houston in the past year and what a mystery they had been. Traveling to Houston for what I thought would be routine work trips had sent me on a puzzling, difficult, often dark journey I never planned on taking. It led me to amazingly transformative experiences I never imagined having. I had been on a journey of memories and enthralling experiences I couldn't predict, comprehend, or control. *Not for the faint of heart, to be sure.*

While sitting on my bench and pondering the past year's events, an unexpected vision appeared in my mind. I saw my father tripping and stumbling along down an empty street like a back-alley drunk. My father, a drunk? This was more than strange because my father was far too pious to touch the stuff. Still, there he was in my vision, looking horribly dirty and frail as he staggered along, a good fifty pounds lighter than I had ever seen him.

His shirt was untucked. His pants were torn and soiled at the crotch. His shoes were scuffed and covered with mud. His hair hung long and dirty over his eyes. He hadn't shaved in weeks. His hands were bent, bloody, and broken. His finger-nails were black with dirt. I could almost smell the stench of his odor. He was mumbling to himself as he staggered along. I could hear he was cursing himself under his breath. He looked so pathetic there was no way I could feel a hint of anger or violence towards him.

I could tell that he was desperately trying to make his way to the safety of heaven because he was facing the last of his dying days. To his great horror, his best, most brilliant, and beautiful talents would never be enough to get him there. No matter how grand and glorious he had worked to be, he could not save himself.

That is when my mom burst into the vision. She arrived with a thunderous *ka-boom!* She was like the birth of a star exploding in the heavenly universe. She wore a white dress. Her hair was a flowing, beautiful dark brown like when she was young. Her countenance blazed bright with soulful strength and overwhelming compassion.

She sprinted toward my father, threw her arms around him, and held him as if she had not seen him in a lifetime. She gently combed his dirty, matted hair from his eyes with her fingers and then gazed deeply into them. She poured out kisses on his face as if they flowed from an endless stream of love.

My father buckled under the weight of her embrace, but she caught him so he wouldn't fall. Still, his withered body shook, and his boney shoulders heaved up and down as he began to sob. His tears became a long dark river, and he bellowed his cry of shame as the veneer of his self-importance washed away into the endless ocean of her grace.

This surprise vision left me as peacefully as it had come. I listened to the birds sing and felt the warmth of the afternoon.

I thought of the elderly woman from Glenlea Street and her question, "You lost, honey?"

I chuckled to myself as I looked at the tiger's-eye; it was still on my father's grave.

No, ma'am. I am not lost.

I found the little fisherman inside of me.

He is more alive than ever.

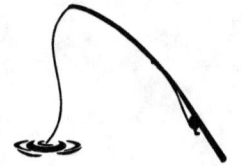

EPILOGUE

IT'S BEEN THREE YEARS since I made those trips to Houston. What I experienced in the cemetery taught me to see my life and the lives of others with more understanding. I also found a longing to know more.

What do we do with our longing?

For me, I am prone to take a road trip.

Early before dawn on a Saturday, I took off in the general direction of Wyoming and Colorado. It was late in the fall, so I left my motorcycle in the garage and took my pickup truck. I wound up in Yellowstone National Park, where I saw bison and a grizzly mother with her cub. Taking my time, I sat beside meandering mountain rivers watching fly fisherman sweep their lines back and forth in arching casts to artfully set the fly down into the river to catch cutthroat trout. The way they worked to entice the fish made me think of Mr. Hargis and I smiled.

From Yellowstone, I made my way to Cheyenne. I went to the city's historic Lions Park to view the sunrise. Mom had taken me there as a boy so I could fish in the lake. I stood at the water's edge and took a selfie with the lake and sunrise in the background.

Click!

Another memory captured as treasure.

From Cheyenne, I headed south toward Boulder. The road began to twist as the rolling grasslands gave way to the foothills of the Rocky Mountains. Cottonwood trees lined the road. Their leaves were the fall colors of tawny brown and gold, the same colors you would see in a tiger's-eye. Then the cottonwoods gave way to spruce and pine evergreens, and quaking aspens, whose leaves shimmered in the sun like yellow and gold glass hanging from the tree limbs by invisible thread. I often stopped to sit on my truck's tailgate, viewing the spectrum of fall colors. There were pinks and reds and various shades of orange, yellow, gold, and brown. Every distinct variation was set perfectly in place — like a finger-painting made by the hand of God.

I was taking it all in when my phone rang. It was my cousin Bryan, the one who had called to tell me my father had died. He had found a bracelet that had belonged to Vesta. On the bracelet was a keepsake with my name on it. He told me that Vesta got a new keepsake to put on her bracelet each time a grandchild was born. When I heard this, I was taken aback and felt mildly stunned. I had never known Vesta to be thoughtful and caring in such a grandmotherly way.

On the way to Boulder, I stopped to have lunch with a long-lost cousin from my mother's side of the family. She and I had not seen one another in fifty years. We shared many of the same memories, but not all of them. A bit older than me, she remembered things I was not old enough to understand. She remembered our grandfather to be domineering, narcissistic, and an unfaithful husband to our grandmother. Our grandmother suffered years of hand-wringing anxiety as a result.

It's natural to guard our memories as if they are the God-told truth and we are the lord of their keeping. Then we can make judgments about who is good or who is bad. We all do it, especially when we are young and fragile. But growing up requires that we recognize there is so much more to know about people and more about ourselves.

Doesn't good and evil cut through the heart of us all?

After lunch with my cousin, I drove up the twisty switchbacks to the top of Flagstaff Mountain to take a stroll. It was late afternoon. The air was cool, and filled with the scent of pine. Everything was quiet — like an abbey. I noticed a footpath and casually followed it deeper into the trees. It was a well-worn path that led me to an area of craggy granite boulders. The trail circled the boulders, and I noticed how they seemed to change shape and character when I viewed them from different places along the path. Then I looked up and was astonished to see a puny misshapen pine tree growing right out of the top of the granite. Its trunk was bulbous and grew sideways for a few feet until it turned up and became finger-like spindly. The twisted branches grew out from only one side, and its pine needles were oddly spaced. Its roots grew across the top of the boulders until they found a crack of soil where they dived down into the earth.

In wonder, I sat down on one of the boulders.

This tree was living proof of the dignity that grows from hardship.

A few minutes later, I noticed a man standing behind a camera mounted on a tripod. He had his camera trained on the tree, so I moved out of sight for him to capture this moment into a treasure. Then I noticed a second twisted tree growing out of the granite some yards away; it was equally marred and misshapen. There was a woman sitting on a rock with a sketch pad in her lap. She looked up at the second tree repeatedly and then back down to sketch what she saw. Not far from her was a young couple. His arm was around her, and her head rested on his shoulder. College sweethearts from the university in Boulder, I assumed. They locked their eyes intently on the tree as if it conveyed important teaching they would never learn in a classroom.

I felt in good company with these people. We shared a common appreciation for these trees, which through hardship and suffering had grown to be beautiful in a way that made them stand out above the rest.

The trees offered us all a question to ponder.

How will you and I grow through hardship and suffering?

ACKNOWLEDGMENTS

The idea of *Death of a Fisherman* first came during a conversation over coffee with my longtime friend Joey O'Connor. He thought others might be interested in my story and suggested I write a memoir. I was skeptical, but nevertheless, I began to write. I then asked him (maybe coerced him a bit) to apply his exceptional skills to edit the work. Thank you, my friend; your edits and friendship make me a better man.

Thanks to Mark Vaughan. I asked Mark to read each chapter as it developed, always anxious to hear his affirmation. Mark's only response every time was, "Hmmm, interesting. Just keep at it. Don't stop until you're finished." Thank you, Mark. The way you do life teaches me things I need to know.

My wholehearted appreciation goes to Joan Tankersley. Joan and I have known one another since we were teenagers. She is perhaps the most faithfully positive person I have ever met and inspired me throughout the publishing process.

I need to thank my friend John W. Kennedy for his insightful consultations, Anne Goetze for her incredible artistry, Natalie Lauren for spot-on graphic design and interior layout, Jessica Snell for eagle-eyed proofreading, and Drew Tilton for superbly managing the publishing process.

Lastly, I thank my *test readers*, twenty random people who read multiple drafts, then offered their sincere and honest responses. Some of them became good friends in the process. Their input helped me to better understand my audience and myself.

MORE BOOKS BY DAVID ZAILER

Our Journey Home:
Insights and Inspirations for Christian 12-Step Recovery

Starting Point for Recovery:
A Simple 12-Step Guide for Use in Counseling
for Addiction Recovery

When Lost Men Come Home:
A Journey to Sexual Integrity